# PH
# ON
# Y!

# PH
# ON
# Y!

## how I faked my way through life

## Andrea Stanfield

## Prometheus Books

59 John Glenn Drive
Amherst, New York 14228-2119

Published 2008 by Prometheus Books

Inquiries should be addressed to
Prometheus Books
59 John Glenn Drive
Amherst, New York 14228–2119
VOICE: 716–691–0133, ext. 210
FAX: 716–691–0137
WWW.PROMETHEUSBOOKS.COM

12  11  10  09  08     5  4  3  2  1

Library of Congress Cataloging-in-Publication Data

Stanfield, Andrea, 1972–
    Phony! how I faked my way through life / by Andrea Stanfield.
        p. cm.
    ISBN 978–1–59102–655–6 (pbk.)
    1. Stanfield, Andrea, 1972–  2. Impostors and imposture—United States—Biography.
I. Title.

CT9981.C64A3  2008
177'.3092—dc22
[B]                                                            2008030597

Printed in the United States on acid-free paper

# INTRODUCTION

Fake it 'til you make it. Somehow that age-old saying did it for me. I told a lie. That lie opened a door, and I walked in.

I sustained the lie for more than a decade and it became the foundation of my professional life. Eventually I had everything I had always wanted: plenty of success, respect, and moolah—all the things I had counted on to make the lie worth telling.

Somewhere along the way, though, I started struggling with myself. I realized that the lie had opened the door, but I felt that I had worked hard and earned the ultimate success on my own.

For some reason I needed cleansing and vindication or I would no longer be able to enjoy the fruits of my labor. I became the person I thought I had to pretend to be. I was "making it"—but was unable to stop "faking it." The only thing that could release me from the lie was the truth, which seemed simple enough, but the lie had been perpetuated over so many years that it served as the groundwork for who I had become. The truth became a giant monkey wrench that sat by, waiting to be tossed into my life. The truth became the one thing that made me doubt myself. The truth was the one thing that scared me, as the lie had entangled itself throughout my circle of family, friends, and co-workers. The lie hadn't hurt anyone, but the truth could hurt *everyone*. That realization made perpetuating the lie logical and rational—but it didn't make it easy.

I read a statistic once that said 40 percent of people fudge on their résumés. I suppose that's not very surprising, and I am certain that percentage includes harmless exaggerations such as extending the time spent at a previous employer or inflating a former job title from *telemarketer* to the much more prestigious *customer service representative*. Harmless, really.

My fudge was a bit more chocolaty. I claimed to have a bachelor's degree in business administration from a large university, when the fact is that I have a high school diploma. I knew that any real management role—even entry level—required a degree even to snag an interview. I was twenty-six and in need of big money, and employee background checks were not yet common practice. The situation was ripe for me to misstep. I was young, fearless, driven, and oblivious to the real world and why people took the long road anywhere. Working two jobs never occurred to me, nor did being a stripper or dealing drugs or any other means of making a fast buck. I had goals, after all, and one of them was to make it in business. I wanted success and respect and had an innate desire to become a corporate manager.

In addition to those nifty ideals, I also wanted a sports car, a Rolex, and beautiful clothes. In my mind it was silly to let my lack of education hold me back. I had made straight As throughout high school and skipped college because it seemed as if it would be boring and, frankly, take far too long. I was ready for LIFE, and since I hadn't found it yet I thought I had better try something to get it kick-started.

Most college graduates I met were pompous, bigheaded dumbbells who I felt I could outsmart and outwit any day of the week, anyway. I felt that I deserved more, something I can only attribute to my youthful exuberance and my lack of life experience. I felt life *owed* me.

So I lied.

It happened so easily, really, and I told the lie so many times that sometimes it seemed real even to me. My husband currently works for the firm where I first used my bogus credentials. The management there is clueless to this day. I had many mentors through the years, all of whom would be blown away by my lack of education. My ten-year-old daughter aspires to be like me—she thinks I am a college grad. Somehow, even my own mother thinks I graduated from college. She brags about me a lot, apparently—the first person in the family to obtain a college degree. Only one of my friends knows the truth, and I think my father may have an idea. I sit and imagine each person's reaction to the truth and I get overwhelmed with guilt, humiliation, and regret. I imagine some people claiming they knew, some claiming they don't care either way, and some writing me off for good.

I hold onto the hope that I have been more to people than a name on a college degree. I hope that they can get past the fact that I lied to them. For that lie, I apologize. And for that I hope I am forgiven, if not understood. Lying was wrong, and I gained a lot financially from it, which is even worse, but I hope people can see how I ultimately grew from it and am a different person today. This book will turn my life upside down, and I am afraid of that. But fear can no longer govern my life.

My dad told me once that we get to go around this "whirly-whirl" (his term for a Ferris wheel) only once in life. It is time for me to come clean, face the music, and all of those other clichés that we as humans say to make throwing in the towel sound like fun.

Here I stand at the edge of the high dive, ready to jump, but not sure why. Maybe I have PMS and need to think it through? But I've taken deep breaths before, waited until morning, and counted to eleven. It's time to get real and tell everyone who I really am.

I choose to believe that when the smoke clears, someone will be there. I choose to believe that I am more than a piece of paper.

Don't get me wrong, I have only myself to blame, and whatever repercussions I experience I deserve. I try to place myself in everyone else's shoes, and at the very least I hope my mom feels like smacking me. That would be a healthy, honest response, and from this day forward I am all about the honesty. My personal embarrassment is nothing compared to that of the people who will feel fooled or taken advantage of by my lies. Again, for that I am sorry.

The fact remains, I lied.

# CHAPTER ONE

I'm a phony. The lines between who I am and who I pretend to be are so fuzzy that sometimes even I can't tell the difference. As I have grown older, my conscience bothers me and begs for reasoning where there isn't any left. I've tried to give back all I've gained to ease the constant pressure, but until people have been told the truth I will always be perceived as someone I am not.

Growing older seems to make me think more about what I did, and thinking about how I got here is easier than finding a way out, so let's start there. Maybe I'm just delaying the inevitable, but baby steps are in order because I have a lot to lose. All the clichés such as "growing a conscience" and "older and wiser" are starting to have meaning to me. It hurts my head to wonder how I could have been so stupid only a decade ago. I wonder how I let it get this far. The real kicker is that it gets harder every day.

Ironically, back then I was looking toward the future, but not far enough. Is everyone in their twenties that blind? How many people have told a lie or made a mistake when they were young and then had to live with it the rest of their lives? Prisons must be full of people who took a wrong turn before they were thirty and are only now seeing the whole picture of what they did and what it cost them. How many people get up every day living a lie and look in the mirror wishing everyone could see the real person? There is no "Get Out of Jail Free" card for us.

I suppose I could have given my boss a jingle to say, "Hey, since I am doing such a great job I thought I might as well tell you that I lied about having a degree . . ." That would pretty much have ruined his day, and several other people's as well, and just about guaranteed my immediate termination. That would have affected my family, my friends, my employees, my daughter, and my life. For what? For me to ease my conscience and restore my self-image? It seems a high price to pay even now, and I would have been the only one who benefited.

Does that make it selfish to come clean? Or is that simply my pride justifying itself to my conscience? Success, respect, and money were not good enough reasons to start the lie. I see that now, but do I have a good enough reason to keep it going?

I have tried to search back through my life and find the first instance of my being a phony so that I could map everything out and try to understand how I ended up here. I hoped to discover that I had been dropped on my head as a baby or suffered something equally traumatic that I could blame. Maybe, I thought, my parents were chronic liars and I was a product of my environment. Or maybe I had to hide in my happy (phony) place to get through my childhood.

No such luck. Apparently growing up for me was a breeze. My parents, school, town, and home life were all aces, and although we weren't wealthy, I never wanted for anything. I was an extremely shy child and a loner by all accounts, but I didn't seem to mind. I had some friends I played with on the weekends, but I was just as happy reading alone in my room. I always felt that other kids my age had been too . . . well, *kiddish*. I was a gifted student and worked very hard to please my parents, especially my dad. I was never spanked because all it took to crush me for days was my dad telling me how disappointed he was in me. My parents understood me somehow, the odd little kid that I must have been, and I am grateful for that.

I have an older sister who took center stage back then. She was cute, loud, and good at dancing, singing, and playing the piano.

Needless to say, she received lots of attention. I wasn't good at any of those things, but I liked to draw, and my dad took a special interest in that. I wasn't very talented, but I spent hours drawing comic strip characters on any paper I could find so that I could show my dad my handiwork. The *Peanuts* comics were my favorite, probably because they were so simple in design.

I don't remember the details, but I remember that when I was about seven years old, I realized that I could trace the characters instead of just drawing them freehand. I was amazed at how much better they looked and thought my discovery was about the neatest thing I had ever figured out in my life. I remember taking the tracings to my dad and how he fussed over them. He told me I was going to be a famous artist someday and that he would take the "drawings" to work and hang them next to his desk and tell everyone what a great artist I was.

Looking back, I realize that he was aware that I had traced them, but at the time I didn't think he knew. After all, I thought I was the first person in the world to discover tracing and surely I deserved *some* sort of kudos for that. I accepted his praise for something I had faked and got lots and lots of attention for doing so. I don't remember feeling bad about it at all or worrying that he might find out. I just remember how important I felt and how much less work it was to trace those drawings than it was to create them on my own. I remember my dad's pride and how my heart swelled with love for him. I had found the short road. And nobody got hurt.

Those tracings served as an early lesson, but I'm not here to blame my dad for doing anything more than being either too nice or too busy to call me out at seven years of age. I do, however, wonder if his doing so would have changed anything. I wonder whether, if he had said he was disappointed in me for trying to pass off tracings as my own drawings, I would have been fundamentally reformed forever. And if I were, would that have been a good thing or a bad thing?

Bottom line: It happened, and I learned to work smarter rather than harder (an adage I already understood two decades before ever hearing it). And if truth had to be swept under the mat for a while, well, who cares so long as nobody got hurt?

Let's face it, at seven years of age my thoughts were about as deep as a puddle. I planned to take art lessons and become the artist I pretended to be anyway, so I just had to catch up to my reputation—that's all. That became the story line of my life for the next twenty-five years: Fake it 'til you make it. The problem was that I never thought far enough ahead to make a plan of what to do once I had "made it."

It's difficult to recall what other experiences I had growing up that may have affected where I am today. Looking back, I think most kids lied about one thing or another, and certainly I did my share of that.

Heck, we're taught early on in life that white lies are okay so long as they're all in good fun. In fact, making up nice things could sometimes make people feel good: no harm, no foul. The game Truth or Dare fascinated me, as the Truth questions were always preceded by "If no one would ever find out . . ." That was a no-brainer for me. I'd take the money or have the fun because it's a win-win situation and no one would ever know the difference.

I couldn't fathom any other answer to those questions. There were kids who said they would give the found money back, but I always figured they were lying because they thought God was listening or something.

Maybe I lacked moral fiber, but maybe it's a stupid question to begin with. The reality is that there's always a possibility of being found out, and the questions should be asked that way: "If there was a good chance your dad might find out and be disappointed in you . . ."

I'm betting that my answers—and my life—would have changed dramatically.

When I became a teenager, I acted pretty much as everyone else I knew did. I lied about who I was with and where I was going. I lied about the cigarettes in my bag belonging to someone else. I lied about my age to buy alcohol for myself and my friends. It never occurred to me that I'd get caught. I realize now that I was too stupid to fail and therefore appeared very mature and confident. I used to buy Blue Maui through the liquor store drive-through at the age of sixteen. The same guy sold it to me every weekend.

The following school year he ended up being a substitute teacher for my eleventh-grade history class. He recognized me, of course, but he never said anything. After class we had a good chuckle about it and smoked a cigarette in the stairwell. Not a great lesson to take through life.

I was extremely intellectual at a young age and was able to morph my personality into whatever made the people around me feel most comfortable. The ability to read people and determine their personalities within moments is a gift that I have to this day. I think it came from being a quiet child and watching and listening more than my counterparts. It was this ability that later made me a great actress when I needed to be.

I realized when dealing with my mother's southern family that all I had to do was throw in a "y'all" once in a while, and they thought I was the best thing to hit the South since grits. With my friends I pretended to like dolls or makeup or whatever it was that they liked. My true love was animals, any kind, size, age, whatever. My aunt got a puppy and I held it until it peed all over me. None of my friends or family seemed too interested in that, so I shelved my hopes to work with animals in exchange for what made folks want to know me. I learned how to find people's buttons and push them to make them feel good or to get what I wanted. I could feel their guard go down and I could feel them relax. That in itself is not strange, but what *is* strange is the level of awareness I had at such a young age.

Sometimes I wasn't really doing it to make them feel good so much as I was doing it to see if I could manipulate their perception of me. I chose words carefully and made clear determinations in my mind as I was speaking to elicit the response I desired. It was all a game in which I thought I was smarter than they were and determined what I wanted them to think of me before I did anything. I would listen for clues and then rattle off some story or compliment, true or not, that set them at ease. I somehow knew how infrequently pretty women are told they are pretty by anyone other than the roofers sitting in the parking lot outside the local 7-Eleven. Hearing it from a young girl always made their day and wouldn't soon be forgotten.

There were times, of course, when I misread people, especially when I was younger. I always learned the most from those situations. My mother was a Sunday school teacher, and her class was just down the hall from where I was sent to learn the word of God. My own teacher was discussing the seven days it took God to make the earth. I was puzzled by this, and raised my hand with what I thought was a very educated and sensible question that would really impress her, coming from a nine-year-old: "If God made the world in seven days, and he made people on the sixth day, when did the dinosaurs live?" I remember the look of shock and disgust on my teacher's face. I knew something had gone terribly wrong, but I was unsure what it was. She started yelling at me, right there in Sunday school. She thought I was trying to make a fool out of her in front of the other kids.

My mind was racing. I was sure that I had my facts straight from science class—I could have sworn we had been taught that people didn't live during the dinosaurs' reign. I was stunned silent, and my teacher marched me right down the hall to my mother. I didn't know what was happening.

My mother was embarrassed and ended up taking me home. I spent the rest of the morning there with my dad and rarely had to go to church again. Even now, in my midthirties, I still remember the look on my mother's face, and I still remember feeling guilty for having embarrassed her at church. But just as importantly, I remember the reaction of my teacher when confronted with a question she didn't have the answer to. I saw the flicker of uncertainty that was immediately followed by anger. I suppose what she did was the only way to save face without risking all the other kids' spiritual well-being. I wonder now if any of the other kids saw it for what it was. Probably not—but I still wonder.

Going forward through life, I was much more careful about offering up questions I didn't know the answers to. Being less outgoing made me more observant and less likely to come off as a know-it-all, two more traits that served me well in the future.

There were other blunders in my life, but for the most part I carefully studied people and was able to emulate what they hoped I would be. I suppose that's what con artists do well—set people at ease and then rob them blind. But that isn't why I did it. I did it for fun, and instead of robbing them blind I made them feel good. It felt good to have people want to have me around them because of the things I said or did, even if I wasn't being the real me. I never pondered who I really was. I was so caught up in making every move based on what I thought people expected of me that I never once stopped to think about just being myself. If I had a real persona, it was trapped somewhere inside.

Throughout my childhood people described me as "quiet" or "stoic." I remember that my second-grade teacher was the first person who called me stoic, and at the time I didn't know what it meant. She told me to look it up in the dictionary, so I did. Webster's dictionary defined it as "One apparently or professedly indifferent to pleasure or pain." That sounded like an insult to me, but I didn't mention that to my teacher. I honestly don't think she meant it as an insult. I know now that I rarely showed emotion, and I rarely do to this day, at least not on the same level as most people. I don't squeal or gush or sob or laugh hysterically. I am rather calm, and I am sure that is what my teacher meant that day. I told my dad what she said, and he told me that some people probably just thought I was shy.

Shyness was an interesting concept, and I wrote my teacher's comment off to that. That made sense to me. It is ironic what we will accept as children when we don't understand the true concept. "Shy" sounded much better than "stoic," at any rate, so I went with it.

People's perception of me as shy or stoic later turned into some people thinking I was stuck-up. I was never the first person to say hello or lighten up the room. I always had a sense of everyone staring at me, and through my awkward teenage years I was never quite comfortable in my own skin. I was kind to everyone I met, though, and made friends easily. Like I said, I enjoyed making people feel good, and they appreciated that.

As expected, I managed to fit into many groups of people, no matter their age or lifestyle. My best friend in high school was a cheerleader and prom queen, but I also smoked cigarettes with the burnouts after school and got straight As. I could be anyone—or anything—I needed to be.

Anyone or anything except the real me. *Whoever* that was.

# CHAPTER TWO

I started working at the ripe old age of fourteen. I probably would have started sooner, except those tricky little child labor laws cramped my style. I did, however, run many of my own start-up businesses even as a small child. I made trinkets and sold them to friends and family. I was pretty creative and enjoyed peddling my wares.

One of my more successful ventures was twisting fuzzy pipe cleaners into cute shapes, gluing on eyeballs and clothes, and selling them as little characters I called Squirmies. I made a whole family of characters, complete with names and personalities. I kept them in an old cigar box and carried them to school to sell them. They were a big hit and I made a few bucks. I put all the money I made into buying more supplies to make more Squirmies. Unfortunately the Squirmy demand wore thin, and in the end I just broke even.

Those early experiences taught me that I enjoyed working and making money. I also learned the value of a dollar. I didn't save my money like a little Scrooge, but when I spent it, I made sure it was for something special. My first few jobs in high school were the usual run-of-the-mill stuff, but from each one I took valuable lessons that helped me later in life.

My first real job in life was at a donut shop. I haven't been in one lately, but back then it consisted of a long counter where the geriatrics gathered each morning for their forty-cent cups of coffee. I worked from 5 to 11 a.m. on Saturday and Sunday mornings and had to wear the most hideous uniform ever stitched into one piece. It consisted of a pink and brown (yes, pink and brown) beanie that I had to fasten to the top of my head and a one-piece mid-calf-length jumper. The dress, made of polyester, was also brown and pink. The sleeves had the added bonus of printed brown and pink flowers. It was the mideighties, but my uniform was an obvious hand-me-down from the seventies—and a few sizes too big to boot. Luckily, I worked such an early shift that my friends never saw me.

I took orders from my boss, a German guy, and his wife, whom I never saw. The only other person who worked the same shift was the donut baker. He stayed in the back frying up donuts most of the time. I stayed out front, waiting on customers. Most of the people who came in to get coffee and donuts to go were crabby, but the regulars who sat at the counter were pretty nice. Coffee was forty cents a cup at the counter, with no free refills. Most of the old guys would pay the forty cents, tip me ten cents (two quarters and "keep the change"), drink their cup of coffee, and leave. I learned very quickly that if I topped off their cups before they finished them and didn't charge them for the refill, they would pay their forty cents for the original cup and tip me the ten cents *plus* another quarter. I figured I was just warming up their coffee, not providing a refill, so they got a bottomless cup of coffee for the bargain price of seventy-five cents.

There were no security cameras in the donut shop, and I doubted that even my penny-pinching boss could determine how many cups of coffee should have been paid for by how many coffee beans were gone. Besides, the regulars loved me and kept coming back every week. No harm, no foul—and I learned how to make my customers happy with a little extra service. They felt special, tipped me a little extra, and kept coming back for more. Nobody got hurt.

I eventually tired of that job and decided to apply for a position at a newly opened breakfast restaurant about a mile from my house. I applied on a Saturday morning, and the charming Italian owner put me to work that same day. I worked only on weekend mornings because I was fifteen and still in school.

The owner was a flirty thirty-something man whose wife was pregnant with twins. He was all hands, and even though I was only fifteen, he was always hugging me or kissing me on the cheek or saying how pretty I was. I didn't think much of it at the time, since he seemed to do it to all the waitresses and even did it when his wife stopped by for breakfast.

One morning he kissed me on the cheek and asked if he could kiss me on the lips. I was taken by surprise and laughed and told him no, figuring he was just kidding. He laughed it off and I thought the subject was dropped. About twenty minutes later he asked me to go down to the basement and get some food from the freezer. He stored all the food and supplies in the basement, and he was always sending me down to the freezer to get more meat or whatever else we needed upstairs. I turned to go and felt him pat me on the behind. I was pretty mature at fifteen, and bells were going off in my head at this point. I knew he was out of line, but I didn't know what to do about it. I mean, this guy was my boss, so I headed off down to the freezer without looking back.

I got the food he had asked for and turned around to head back up the stairs—and there he was, coming down the last few steps. There was no one else in the basement, and I felt my senses go on high alert. I stopped in my tracks and couldn't say a word. He said he had come down to apologize to me for asking for the kiss. I stammered that it was okay and tried to walk around him to the stairway. He touched my arm and said since I forgave him would I give him a hug. My brain was on fire but I didn't know what to say, so I gave him a hug. I let go, but he didn't, and then he asked me if I knew what oral sex was (he didn't use those words). I felt him start to push down on my arms, and that was what it finally took for me to gather my senses enough to act.

I pulled away, ran up the stairs, ran out of the restaurant, and raced all the way home. Both of my parents were there, and I gave them a teary explanation of what had happened. My father stormed out of the house—I assume to go find the pervert—and returned an hour later.

I never asked what happened, and I never went back to that place. The last I heard, the restaurant was still in existence, so maybe the owner learned a lesson that day. I know that I learned everything is not always as it seems. I learned to be watchful of anyone who is too nice for no apparent reason. I learned that I was a girl in a man's world and I had to be careful about that. I made a promise to myself that I would make it in the working world on my own, not by doing disgusting favors for the boss. Besides, I had dear old Dad to back me up if anyone crossed the line.

After my short-lived experience as a waitress, I found myself job-less once again, so I applied to be a clerk at a craft store. I got the position and worked for a woman who hated her job. My job was easy enough: stocking shelves, running the cash register, and directing customers through the store. I worked with other kids my age, and we had a pretty good time. Our boss, however, was one of the unhappiest women I have ever met. She was mean, rude, condescending, and flat-out boorish. She made our hair stand on end whenever we heard her clip-clopping down the aisle. If she wanted to yell at you, she wouldn't wait until the customer walked away. She would just cut into you, swearing and all, in front of whoever happened to be standing there at the time.

Certain things sent her over the edge, and I figured those out early on in our relationship. This helped me to get yelled at less often. She wanted us to be on time, to be dressed appropriately, to be efficient, and to make no mistakes. I worked hard to avoid attracting her attention and was pretty successful at it. If an employee asked for a vacation day she regularly denied the request, and she fired employees for calling in sick more than once. So I attempted neither of those things. She preached about work ethic and the good old days, and I see now that she must have been frustrated by all the young whippersnappers working there just so we could put gas in the cars our parents had bought us.

Looking back, I feel bad for her, but at the time I just loathed her. She taught me some valuable lessons, though—including work ethic, dedication, and how to do a good job no matter how menial a task seemed.

I managed to keep pretty busy between school and work, and I still maintained something of a social life through middle and high school. I always dated older boys because they seemed to understand me better. They were impressed that I had a job and a car and could talk about things other than clothes and school. My parents didn't seem to mind that my boyfriends were older and liked most of them. I remember only one time when my father didn't like my boyfriend, and that was because he had long hair. He was an artist, though, and I was fascinated by that.

He had already graduated high school and was working at a local art shop. I knew my father didn't like his hair, but I kept hoping he could see past that. My father's opinion meant a lot to me. I kept pushing the issue, and one Christmas my father suggested that my boyfriend come over for dinner. Not only that, but he had gotten him a gift! I couldn't believe my ears!

I rounded up my boyfriend and made him get dressed up, and we headed to my parents' house. We had a nice dinner before gravitating to the living room to open the gifts. We all opened a few presents, and

21

then my father handed one to my boyfriend. I was so excited, and my boyfriend was, too. He ripped open the package and pulled out . . . a shiny new pair of scissors.

My parents cracked up, but I was horrified. My boyfriend didn't know what to say, so he just sat there, stunned. I told my father how mean I thought it was, but I am not sure if he heard me over the laughter. My boyfriend and I broke up soon afterward. There is simply no recovering from a moment like that.

That night I learned that people—even my father—were hung up on appearances. People could choose either to conform and make the road ahead a little easier for themselves or to portray on the outside who they really were on the inside and risk isolating themselves from other groups of people forever.

Could you change how you look on the outside and still be true to who you are internally? I didn't know it then, but I would never date a guy with long hair again. I wanted my father's approval, and I figured, Why start out with something he would never overcome? I couldn't change him, so instead I changed a little something about myself . . . one more time.

# CHAPTER THREE

I was graduating from high school and ready to be all grown up. I had no interest in normal teenage things such as proms and sports. Heck, I had experienced those in the ninth and tenth grades and found them to be for babies. I never even had my picture taken for the yearbook. I was ready to live life—*real* life.

Of course, college was out of the question for me, because that would merely delay my success, and I hadn't yet learned that a bachelor's degree was a prerequisite to all of my goals. My mother, on the other hand, had a different point of view: I needed to continue my education. *Period.* She was so adamant that I eventually stopped talking to her about it because no excuse I could come up with was ever good enough.

My point of view was quite different. I had been working at various low-paying jobs since I was fourteen, and now it was time to get a *real* job. I had excelled at math in school, and the thought of being an accountant sounded professional and exciting. I had a boyfriend who was five years my senior, and I moved in with him shortly after graduation. His dad was paying our rent so long as he stayed in college, so it was a great deal for us both.

I got a job doing accounting work for an attorney, and it turned out to be terrific. I learned a lot about business finance. Nothing about the position was over my head. Someone was always willing to show me the ropes or help me with any problems I encountered. I worked very hard and was earning nearly $35,000 a year by the time I was twenty-two, when others my age were earning $12,000 to $15,000 at jobs they hated.

I worked with several other girls in the office, a couple of whom were in college trying to advance their careers. Once they graduated they were promoted—and that's when I began to realize that this education thing might have been more important than I'd realized after all. There were times when I felt left behind, but rather than look at my shortcomings as my own doing, I felt cheated. Who, after all, deserved success more than I?

But what to do about it? That was the question. I was helping my boyfriend with his college homework every night and working full-time during the day. We rented a house that we treated as our own and had two dogs to care for. I was already pretending to be a family and pretending to be too busy to do what I knew I should do. I was pretending to be all grown up and pretending that my little bookkeeping job was a career worth sacrificing for.

I had gotten a taste of real life and I loved it. I loved the responsibility and dressing like a grown-up businesswoman every day. I loved working in an office. I even loved the commute.

Unfortunately, the days marched on and eventually became mundane. I really wanted to be married, which was the next logical step in my fantasy world, but my boyfriend was reluctant to make a commitment. He was living a whole other life at college and beginning to drift away, at least emotionally. He kept suggesting that I might like college, telling me how he wanted to marry someone who was his equal—subtle hints that were beginning to find their way home.

In the spirit of being what I thought he wanted me to be, I decided to take a stab at the wonderful world of higher education. I enrolled in summer school, bought my books, changed my work schedule, and prepared to blow the doors off this whole education thing.

I chose some cool classes, including science and marketing, in which I got to make my own commercial. I remember wondering how these classes could possibly cost $400 each. Unfortunately for me, I tested into extremely difficult arithmetic courses such as Calculus II, but I decided to postpone those for the next semester.

My classes were mostly in the evenings, and although I managed to get there after work, I found myself daydreaming about being home with my boyfriend. I ran through fantasy conversations in my mind about how thrilled he and his parents were that I was going to school. Ridiculous, I know, but no less the truth.

The one thing I remember most from my brief college career was one of my professors. He was a high-powered manager at some bank during the day and a professor at night. He would be teaching us something and get sidetracked with some story about something that had happened in his career. His stories were fascinating. They involved huge amounts of money that seemed mind-boggling at the time, making major decisions, attending board meetings, and other real-world big-shot stuff. I envied him for getting to do those things every day and couldn't wait to have my shot at it.

I was working full-time and going to class part-time, and it was beginning to show. It seemed as if I was falling into a rut very early in life. Then, one Saturday morning, I received a call that changed my life. My sister's son had nearly smothered in his crib and he was in the hospital, near death. My mother had called me from the hospital hours after it had happened. She had tried to reach me several times, but that was before cell phones were commonplace, and I had been out all morning shopping for shoes.

When I got the news, I jumped into my car and sped over to the hospital. I remember distinctly that my foot was trembling so hard I could barely keep steady pressure on the gas. All I knew at that point was that my nephew was on life support, and I feared the worst. I had heard the same fear in my mother's voice.

I finally made it to the hospital and somehow found my way to where my family had gathered. My sister was crying and totally over the edge, my mother was about the same, and my father was sitting quietly but buzzing with anxiety. I felt worst of all for my brother-in-law. He was catatonic, in shock. He didn't speak a word for three weeks following that day. I tried to gather as much information as I could about what had happened and what state my tiny nephew was in.

The news was grim. My brother-in-law had found the baby unconscious and had done mouth-to-mouth until the ambulance arrived. My nephew was on a breathing machine and the doctors were trying to determine if his brain was still functioning. They doubted it.

He was five months old and he lived three more days, but finally they had to pull the plug due to organ failure and brain damage. I watched some of the tests for brain activity and will never be able to forget them. One test involved opening up his eye with their fingers and touching his eyeball with a cotton ball. No response, no brain activity. Seems pretty basic, but at the time it made me sick. It was a test in which the results were clear, and it made the bleakness of the situation undeniable. Watching the doctor rub the cotton on his eye made me want to scream. No one told me the eye should respond, but I knew. When it didn't even flinch, my heart sank. I knew at that moment he was not going to make it.

We had a couple of hope-filled days as his little body kept fighting to stay alive, but eventually the lack of brain function started to wear on his organs. Blood appeared in his diapers, and his kidneys were failing. The time had come to make the decision.

My brother-in-law still couldn't speak or even comprehend what was going on, but the family made the decision. As my sister cradled her son in her arms, the doctors removed his breathing tube. It took about an hour for him to pass quietly. I held his tiny hand during that hour, and it tore me to pieces. Everything around me suddenly wound to a stop. I hung on every breath I watched him take, knowing that each one might be his last. The slight rise and fall of his back eventually stopped. I wanted to end all the pain, everyone's pain, and hit the rewind button back to four days ago. I wanted to change the past and alter the future. I would have given anything—even my own life—to change what was happening before my very eyes. But no one, I realized, has the power to make deals like that.

The funeral was held a few days later. My sister was medicated beyond any ability to rationalize what was happening and wore a black veil to cover her face. I was shocked that the casket was open but was grateful to give my nephew one last kiss.

I rode from the funeral to the graveyard in a black limousine with my nephew's miniature coffin in the backseat. In the seat next to me was my three-year-old niece, unaware of what was happening. She would go through life never knowing her brother.

When we arrived at the cemetery, I tried to remain strong for anyone who needed comforting. They put his casket in the hole in the earth and everyone began to sing "Jesus Loves Me." I finally broke down and began to sob. To this day I can't listen to the lyrics of that song without crumbling.

I left the graveyard with a different outlook on life. My priorities had suddenly changed, and the little things in life that I had previously taken for granted seemed to be all that mattered.

The next several weeks remain a blur to me, but I know that my nephew's death became my excuse to fail at school and to alter the course I was on. My sister was going down in flames, my parents were aging by the second, and no one could stop the pain or reverse what had happened. I had never experienced a loss like that in my life. I felt totally out of control. I felt that nothing else in my life was important.

Everything I cared about before that day seemed frivolous, selfish, and arbitrary. I felt that I had to escape the sadness somehow. My boyfriend suggested that we take a cross-country trip to get away. He wasn't taking summer courses and I no longer cared about mine, so we began making plans. Three months and three thousand miles of escape: literally, time and space.

We bought a $600 van, packed up the dogs, and took off. We drove from Ohio to Georgia and then out to California before returning home. Along the way, we ate canned food, showered in public restrooms, and lived off the land. We visited national parks and saw many amazing sights. It would have been a dream come true for most people, but I hated it. I suppose the trip would have been better had I not felt so empty inside. I wore glasses instead of my contacts and dressed like a hippie. I made it through the ordeal by pretending to be someone else. How deep is the hurt when even the Grand Canyon seems mundane?

Throughout the trip, my boyfriend and I fought constantly. I think I was tired of playing a role, of being whoever he wanted me to be. My pain was real and I couldn't hide it just to make him feel better. He acted as if I should get over it, but I couldn't. I couldn't pretend to have a good time, and I couldn't pretend that I was enjoying camping. I just wanted to go home, and after days of nonstop bickering, we finally headed back.

I never returned to my college classes, and my transcript reflects the failing grades I earned that summer. I've seen my transcript once in my life since then. The paper brings back a flood of pain and memories of a time I thought I had successfully buried.

Despite its shortcomings, the trip did do me *some* good. Afterward, I began to feel emotionally stronger. At the very least, I had learned that I didn't like camping or going through life on a shoestring. I learned that I would never enjoy being poor, and I got to see some areas of the country where I would have liked to have lived. I don't think anyone in my family ever truly healed from the loss of my nephew, but life moves on and the sun keeps coming up each day.

My sister sued the crib's manufacturer and eventually was awarded a $10 million settlement. The litigation took a couple of years, but in the end, the company was found at fault for designing an unsafe crib. I sat through two weeks of the trial and watched as the attorneys debated the price of a human life. I watched as the president of the company said that *only* nine babies had accidentally died in its cribs over the past twenty years. Yes, *only* nine.

In those hours of testimony I saw a side of corporate America I had never known existed. I saw that business was a *thing*. It's an entity without feelings, and it's driven by a single goal: profits. Whatever got in the way of those profits would be dealt with severely. Anything else would be left by the wayside. Apparently the first eight dead babies hadn't put a dent in the company's long-term plans. Here in the courtroom sat the figurehead, telling us all how irrational we were being because we were worried about one tiny little life. The most chilling part of the president's testimony is that he actually believed what he was saying. He was a piece of this machine, this corporation, and couldn't see past his own retirement nest egg.

The attorneys wore their power suits and argued the case, as they had done countless times before. In the end they would both be paid for doing their jobs, and we would still be facing life without my nephew.

The coldness was palpable, and I lost all respect for the corporate machine that day. In any given situation it was every person for himself, and if you try to mess with the machine, its attorneys will take you down. No matter how great your emotional loss, the corporate machine perceives any financial loss as much greater. The president of that company showed his lack of compassion and couth that day. Luckily, the jury did not.

I watched the jurors gasp as my sister's attorney used a doll to depict how my nephew was hanging with his face pressed against the side of the mattress, his head caught in the bars, smothering and kicking the wall, to no avail. I cried when my brother-in-law testified that he had heard the kicking and thought it was a salesman at their door and ignored it. The opposing attorney asked him if he hadn't seen in the crib assembly instructions that the screws should be checked periodically for loosening. I watched as they cross-examined my sister and asked her if maybe she shouldn't have vacuumed the room so much, since the vacuum can cause vibrations that could loosen the screws.

The insensitivity of the crib manufacturer's defense was mind-boggling. I heard a juror whisper "Jesus Christ" in utter disgust when it was disclosed that the "engineer" who designed the crib wasn't an engineer at all, but rather a close friend of the president of the firm, someone who had needed a job. He had built the crib based on other models he saw at the local baby store.

When asked why he didn't call for the use of screws that don't loosen, he said that he didn't know such a thing existed. He was as stunned as everyone else when my sister's attorney pointed out that those types of screws had been used on other models of cribs made by the same company—higher-end models designed by real engineers. I was appalled, as was the jury, which didn't take long to deliberate.

My sister's goal was to put the company out of business, which she eventually did. She was awarded $10 million, and shortly after the corporation filed for bankruptcy and subsequently disappeared from the map. That was front-page news in our town even though she never saw a penny. Her life was shattered, her mental health questionable every day for the rest of her time on earth, and she was left with a $1 million liability settlement from the insurance company. A third of that went to the attorneys, and half of the remainder went to her husband, from whom she was by then divorced. My sister ended up with little more than a couple hundred thousand dollars in exchange for all of her bitterness, sadness, anger, and doubt in a higher power.

Oh and one more thing: She became *famous*. The newspaper reported that she had been awarded $10 million, and people came out of the woodwork to claim their "rightful" portion of that. Gifts, food, flowers, letters, phone calls, and teddy bears poured out of the community and onto our family's front porches. Everyone was suddenly a lost cousin or a godparent or a close friend. A girl with whom we had attended high school but otherwise hardly knew committed suicide and bequeathed her infant daughter to my sister via a handwritten suicide note. Luckily the child's grandmother stepped forward and took the child in, but the extent of the insanity was clear. Our town was blinded by that $10 million headline, and my sister became the target for every greedy, bleeding soul around.

She adjusted the best she could as we attempted to move on with our lives. My boyfriend graduated from college and—*big surprise*—suddenly became better than I. I began to see the difference in his attitude as he made it clear that I should attempt to finish school if I ever wanted to become a permanent member of his family.

He began fraternizing with pretty girls at work and having "dinners" with clients I "couldn't possibly relate to." Imagine his embarrassment if someone asked me where I had gone to school! I was amazed how quickly his ego grew after he received that simple piece of paper. It didn't seem to matter that I had done his homework for him. Even his family began to turn on me. His mother conveniently forgot my name a couple of times during idle conversations, and that signaled the slow, steady beginning of our decline as a couple.

The relationship soured mostly because I got tired of changing myself to please him, but his new college grad friend—whom he was teaching to play the guitar—didn't help. She never seemed as interested in playing guitar as she was in playing around, and so it went. My boyfriend and I argued a lot, and he eventually got someone else pregnant, which I learned when the other woman called to tell me herself one evening when he wasn't home. She said he knew about the pregnancy but hadn't told me yet.

When he returned home that night, I asked him if there was anything he wanted to tell me. I told him that he had one chance to come clean and tell me the truth. One chance. He said that he had no idea what I was talking about. So I left my so-called life, rented a place of my own, and bought a dog. And once again I found myself alone and in need of a brand-new start.

# CHAPTER FOUR

I needed a new beginning, so I switched jobs and became the Gal Friday to a guy who used television infomercials to sell a medical pain relief device. The company sold $2 grill igniters disguised as $80 medical units to unsuspecting old people, who then used the devices to shock themselves in the hope that it would ease their aches and pains. The devices looked like fat little syringes and could be activated using one hand. The shock was delivered via a metal tip that could be used anywhere on the body.

These little devices packed a surprisingly potent punch, too. I tried one on my own arm and never let anyone near me with one again. It alarmed me that arthritis might actually hurt worse than shocking myself with this little wonder. I was not looking forward to growing older.

The people I worked for were shysters who compromised all of their ethics on a daily basis. But boy, oh boy, did they get *rich*! I was in charge of opening the mail, counting the money, and playing the role of my boss's biggest fan. He had Short Man Syndrome, but luckily for him, I understood (my dad having been a sufferer), and I made him feel ten feet tall every chance I got. He was basically my height, and I am no giant, so I wore flat shoes and hung everything at eye level for him. I even stopped adding body to my hairstyle to make myself appear shorter. He was probably never able to put his finger on why he liked me around so much, but that was okay, so long as it worked.

The job was a blast, but what we were doing weighed on my conscience. Every night after the infomercials aired, hundreds of elderly people called in and ordered their very own shock devices. Many of them wrote letters that raved about how the device had cured them of their pain. Others wrote or called to say it was a scam.

If customers were unhappy, we always refunded their money. The truth is that most of the old people didn't bother to return the things, even though they didn't work, so my boss got rich on their lack of initiative. To justify my involvement, I clung to the letters from the people who actually said they felt better, if only in their minds. I hung their testimonials all around the office, hoping that they showed everyone that we weren't all just a bunch of scammers taking old people's money. But I think we all knew better.

I watched my boss trade his soul for the almighty dollar. I saw him relish in the attention and thoroughly enjoy being the boss. That's when I first fell in love with the idea of being in charge.

I admired how people treated him, and I totally understood why he enjoyed it so much. He would hand me cash bonuses and buy everyone lunch on a whim. He didn't do it to help us; he did it because it made him feel good about himself. He did it because he could. I wanted to be able to do those kinds of things for people one day. Ironically, I wanted to be able to do those things for the same reason that he did: to make me feel good about myself. I guess it's a way of showing off, a way of letting everyone know you can afford it because you are a big shot. He trusted me implicitly. I'm not sure why, nor am I sure that that was something to be proud of. But I was.

I kept working for the firm because I was paid well and treated with respect. I felt like a big shot, too, sometimes, and was privy to many private meetings and major business decisions, even if I was there only to take minutes. The dollar figures discussed were unbelievable, and many decisions seemed rash and unfounded—but at the same time genius. I saw my boss living the good life and promised myself that I would have the same kinds of material things someday, although without hurting people to get them.

I drove his custom Mercedes to the airport to pick up celebrity actors for the infomercials, and I felt wonderful doing it. I had never even been in a Mercedes before, and driving one made me feel like someone special, even if it wasn't mine. After all, no one else on the road knew it didn't belong to me. I relished pulling up at the airport and imagined that everyone was staring at me and wondering what I did for a living. I imagined the women were wishing they were me and the men were wishing they were with me—all because of a car. I thought of myself as a different person because of what I was driving. Unfortunately, it also made me hate driving my own car, which up until that time hadn't seemed so bad.

I got my first cell phone at a time when they were still pretty rare. My boss insisted that I have one so he could reach me if he needed anything quickly. It weighed about two pounds, but I loved it because it made me look "cutting edge." I didn't know anyone else who had one, except for my boss, so I figured it made me look pretty rich, too. I didn't have anyone to call, but frankly that didn't bother me too much.

Business was going well for the company, but the Feds finally put a stop to that. One day I was driving the Mercedes and hoping for my cell phone to ring, and the next I was face down on the floor while gun-bearing federal agents in full riot gear confiscated all the computers and all of our inventory. The company had made several medical claims without FDA approval, something the government frowns upon. That ended *that* "career." I never even got my last paycheck.

During my tenure with the company, I had begun accumulating some debt. My first credit card was a Discover card with a $1,000 limit. I got the application in the mail, and although I didn't need the credit, I was flattered that I had been "chosen" and applied. I felt ten feet tall when I was informed that I had been accepted.

I soon began using the card all the time. I felt like a real grown-up when I bought things and laid that little piece of plastic on the counter. I paid my bill on time, and, sure enough, more offers for credit poured in.

By my early twenties I had managed to amass several thousand dollars' worth of debt. I had spent the money on furniture, clothes, and jewelry. I was always able to make my monthly payments, and my credit report must have appeared impeccable for someone my age. I was unable to save money because of the monthly payments, but I enjoyed the things I bought and didn't have the foresight to worry about it.

Soon enough I found myself stalled again in life, with no real direction. I had a new boyfriend who helped me pass the time, but he wasn't ready to do more than play house, and I wanted more. He had an idea of how life was supposed to be, but unfortunately his plans didn't include settling down and getting married for several more years, and that just wasn't going to work for me.

My sister, who was healing slowly, suggested that she and I move away—somewhere far from home—and start fresh. With no job, a losing relationship, and little hope for the future, I thought it seemed like a good idea.

We finally decided upon Florida, on a very pretty beach. I had always dreamed of vacationing there but never had the opportunity. Now, all of a sudden, I had the chance to live there. It was a dream come true.

My sister agreed to foot the bill for the move so long as I got a job as soon as I arrived. No problem with that. She even helped me pay off the debts that I had accumulated. Poof, and they were gone. Paying off my debts should have been a major accomplishment, even with my sister's help, but I barely even acknowledged it at the time. I was so used to everything happening easily and had so little understanding of the reality of debt that it seemed like an everyday occurrence to me. You create debt, you get rid of debt, no matter how.

So Sis and I landed in Florida with my dog in tow. It was a little slice of heaven for a midwesterner—a beautiful place with zero ex-boyfriends, zero family, and zero *anyone* who knew me. At the ripe old age of twenty-four, I felt I could finally get my life on track and start making my millions. But where and how to begin?

I rented a cute little cottage on the beach. My sister got a place not too far away, and together we had a ball. Tourism was the town's major industry, so we had plenty of bars, grills, and other fun places to hang out. The weather was hot, but the breezes off the ocean were everything I had imagined. I couldn't understand why people would live anywhere else. I felt as if I was on the best vacation of my life . . . every day of the year.

I eventually landed a job as a bookkeeper at an engineering firm and learned how to do payroll and manage a 401(k) plan. My résumé was very accurate at the time—not even the slightest hint of exaggeration. I was making much less money than I had at my previous job in Ohio, but I was told that that was because of Florida's sagging economy.

Luckily, my rent was pretty reasonable, and with my credit cards paid off, I didn't have anything else weighing me down. Comfortable in my life for the first time in years, I set out to meet Mr. Right so that I could start claiming my piece of the Great American Dream.

For every potential suitor I met, I had developed a larger story of my background. I didn't think it was too out of the ordinary to lie about what I did for a living, even if some of the stories were real doozies.

I finally met, fell in love with, and eventually married a man with whom I would have my only child faster than you can say "I do." In retrospect, I picked him for three reasons: (1) he was funny; (2) he was blue-collar and therefore the polar opposite of my last long-term boyfriend, who had become so much better than I; and (3) my beach cottage had flooded and he conveniently had a room for rent. Not very good reasons for joining with someone in holy matrimony, but I wasn't exactly thinking everything through back then.

After moving into his home, I quickly learned that, the laws of nature being what they were, animals in captivity will mate, and we ended up falling for each other. Since we were already living under the same roof and our dogs got along famously, I did what I rationalized every other woman in my shoes would have done: I lied. I told him that I worked as a CPA (my particularly favorite doozy), and I thought I had gotten away with it. But I was outed just before we were married. Some members of his extended family owned a private investigation firm, and it didn't take them long to find out the truth.

When he heard the news, he confronted me about it, and I came clean, expecting the worst. But he ended up marrying me anyway, reinforcing the notion that nobody gets hurt from little white lies. I soon got pregnant and ended up hating him before I gave birth. We wound up in a bitter divorce and custody battle shortly thereafter. So much for the Great American Dream.

I found pregnancy to be an amazing experience: it was like living hell. And childbirth wasn't one of my finer moments either. Nothing about either experience felt "normal" to me. To my knowledge, I never glowed or nested. I did, however, swell up like a balloon and ate cardboard boxes at work because I thought they smelled delicious. I had morning sickness all day and heartburn all night for nine solid months.

For the first few months of my pregnancy my marriage was still going okay, and that made everything seem bearable. During month five or six my husband began to worry that he had given up too much freedom too soon and started trying to reclaim his manhood. He had lots of single friends and an alcohol addiction he carries to this day. Not a good combination. Some nights he didn't come home until very late; others, not at all. When he did come home, he often smelled like perfume or whipped cream. Honest to God. He prided himself on being the life of the party, which ironically had seemed so much fun when we were dating, but in marriage it quickly turned into a nightmare.

I felt helpless, crabby, and sad. Mostly crabby. I was getting larger every day and the vomiting was relentless. Every time I bent over my husband would make farting noises with his mouth like I was ripping my pants. The only nice thing he said to me was how great my body *used* to be.

I tried accompanying him a couple of times to the local bars, even though I couldn't drink. I was disgusted by the men who hit on me when he was off flirting with everyone else. These guys would literally offer to buy me a hot chocolate and try to win me over by telling me what a creep my husband was. Sometimes—sitting there like a blimp, tasting vomit in my throat, my feet aching—it seemed surreal. It was as if I was so outside of anything I had ever pictured for myself that my mind wouldn't accept it. I felt something boiling inside. I suppose now that that something was resentment.

I have learned over the years that once unleashed, resentment is very difficult to rein in. It's something that can destroy love. It starts out small but builds on itself quickly. Every time he drank. Every cruel thing he said. Every time he didn't come home. Every time he made me feel bad. By month seven of my pregnancy the boil was rolling and the damage was done. We were about to become a statistic.

During the last few months of my pregnancy, I was introduced to a girl who had gone to high school with my husband and who also happened to be pregnant. She was a couple months further along than I, but she was a lifesaver when it came to passing the time. Her husband was charming, sweet, and extremely handsome. She was gorgeous even when she was pregnant, and they seemed the perfect match. We became easy friends, which made her my only friend since moving to Florida. She let me borrow whatever maternity clothes she had outgrown, and we looked forward to giving birth close together.

Her husband owned a cleaning business and was gone every night working the evening shift. They both drove top-of-the-line SUVs and bought a cute house in the suburbs. She didn't have to work and was able to buy pretty much anything she wanted because of the money her husband was making. I envied her a lot during those days, but she was very kind and never made me feel bad about my situation.

As the holidays approached, she planned a huge New Year's Eve bash at their new home. I was glad to have somewhere to go and be with, since both of us were sore and sober all the time. Shortly after my husband and I arrived, we were munching on appetizers when the telephone rang. She answered it, looked up once, and then hurried off into the other room to take the call. In that one look I saw something devastating. She had turned pale in that instant in a way that only happens when the news on the other end of the line is horrible beyond comprehension.

Things became a blur after that. The party ended abruptly, and my friend was screaming and in tears. All the drunks were trying to figure out what was going on and trying to console her. She shut herself up in a room and wouldn't come out. Her husband left, and at the time I knew that couldn't be a good sign. He hadn't even tried to get her out of the room. We left shortly after and ended up hearing what had happened a few days later.

Her husband didn't own a cleaning business. He had another wife. He spent his nights with her. And he had a fiancée who got all his in-between time. He had been taking money from these two other women in order to fund his marriage to my friend. All three had rings and all three were clueless about the others. The phone call had been from his other wife, who had somehow found out.

When all was said and done, both of the other women sued him for the money he had taken from them, and he went to jail. The authorities came to my friend's house and informed her that she didn't own it. He had simply rented the place and lied.

The nursery she had painted no longer would be there for her unborn baby. The police also confiscated everything they had bought during the year he had been taking the other women's money. They took it all—the TV, the furniture, and all the baby clothes they had bought. I spoke to her on the phone during that time and she kept saying she was okay. She said the only time she cried was when they took the tiny Reeboks she had so looked forward to putting on her little girl's feet.

To make matters worse, rumors were circulating that she had known all about it from the start. I chose not to believe that. Yes, she was a bright girl, but I was there that night when she got the call. I saw her eyes. She had been taken in right along with everyone else. The kicker was that he hadn't taken anything from her. He had taken from the others to give to her.

All in all, the total damages were a little shy of a hundred thousand dollars. Since my friend was the primary beneficiary, she remained a suspect in the ruse for several weeks. The authorities eventually cleared her, but her husband was in prison before she gave birth a couple months later.

They never got back together, even when he got out of prison. He told her that he suffered from bipolar disorder and had done it all because he loved her and wanted to please her. I suppose in the end it was her resentment that was his downfall—resentment over the embarrassment and resentment over the tiny Reeboks her daughter would never wear. No one can recover from that kind of resentment, no matter how good the excuse for doing something may seem.

While it helped distract me for a couple months, even all that drama couldn't keep me from noticing my own faltering marriage. My husband's drinking was out of control, although I couldn't really blame him. It was miserable at home and there was no turning me around. What choice did he have at that point? He was a delivery driver for a huge company and drove his truck onto company property while intoxicated one night. He was fired and became embroiled in a union battle to recover his job. All that did was give him more free time to drink and make fun of how much weight I had gained.

Bad soon turned to worse, and the next couple of months were a blur. I acted quickly and, looking back, harshly. I don't know if it was my raging hormones or that curious demon resentment, but I didn't care about anything except my baby and myself.

My niece was about six years old at the time and had just gotten the Disney movie *Beauty and the Beast*. In the movie there is a scene where Beauty falls off a horse while trying to escape and the Beast has to protect her from wolves that begin closing in. He guards her by hovering over her with his body. Suddenly he seems to change. Even in a cartoon, the change was obvious.

When I saw that scene, I made up my mind that the only thing in life that mattered was my daughter and me. I was going to leave my husband because he was bad for me, and therefore bad for her, but the timing was terrible because I was about to give birth.

Now, I love children, and I love my daughter to death. Nevertheless, childbirth was the most frightening thing I have ever been through in my life. I was terrified of the experience and everything it involved. Just thinking about getting an epidural nearly sent me over the edge. Every mother I ever met told me that once it was time to give birth I would be fine. Maybe I am missing some crucial gene or something, because that never happened for me. I was terrified. It didn't help that my pregnancy had caused my blood pressure to go through the roof and that the doctor said my pelvic opening was too small to allow the baby to continue to cook. I had to be induced.

The one great thing about being induced is that it made the delivery easier to plan for and get everyone we needed involved. Even my mother came to stay for a month to help me out.

We all checked into the hospital bright and early on a Tuesday morning and prepared to bring my daughter into the world. Everyone was in good spirits. Perhaps it wouldn't be so bad after all.

And then reality set in. From seven that morning until ten that night, I wanted nothing more than to crawl in a hole and die.

Early that morning they induced labor and told us it would be a while longer. My mother decided to go grocery shopping and ended up in the emergency room with a broken foot after she dropped a large container of detergent on it.

My ex-husband-to-be came to the delivery room, along with his best friend, and spent 99 percent of the time outside smoking. The doctor showed me a syringe filled with some silver liquid and told me that if I couldn't learn to control my blood pressure through breathing exercises, then he would have to give me a shot. Apparently the shot would make me feel ten times worse than I already did and would haunt me for several days.

What a blast I was having, and it was about to get worse.

A very large nurse, whom I had never seen before and hope never

43

to lay eyes on again, came into the room. My labor pains had already started but were still relatively bearable. I was so focused on trying to avoid the toxic shot that I hadn't really thought about what might come next.

What came next was the epidural.

For anyone who is blissfully unaware of what an epidural is, think of it as a way of numbing the entire lower half of a woman's body by injecting wonder drugs into her spinal cord through a needle the size of a McDonald's soda straw. As if that weren't bad enough, if you move while they're toying with your spinal juices, you could be paralyzed for life.

This was the first time in my life that I remember the real me surfacing in front of people I didn't know. I didn't care at all about what anyone thought about me, what I said, or what I did next. Terror grabbed me by the throat. I can only guess that it was the animal instinct response of flight or fight, and I tried to flee. But Monster Nurse grabbed hold of me just as a contraction brought me crashing to my knees. I swear she chuckled as she hoisted me back into bed.

Since "flight" mode had failed miserably, I launched into my next option. I began kicking and screaming and swearing like a drunken sailor, and it took three nurses to hold me down as they administered the drugs. It was as awful as I had thought it would be—and then some. I had seen it done on television but hadn't realized that they leave the straw in there in case they need to administer more medication later.

Exhausted from the fear and the battle, I grew terrified as I lost all feeling in the lower half of my body.

The epidural wore off after four hours, just in time for the real labor pains to set in, and I watched the doctor and nurses whisper to one another before telling me that they wouldn't be administering any more juice. They said my labor had stalled and more medication would only make matters worse.

Before they could say another word, a labor pain hit me that made the one during my escape attempt seem like a bee sting. I couldn't even scream because I couldn't find any air.

And so it went for the next several hours. No one would stay in the room with me because all I did was yell, swear, complain, and curse for someone to get me more drugs.

By 10 p.m. the doctor left to prepare the operating room down the hall for a C-section, which brought on a brand-new terror. I couldn't fathom that I had gone through all this pain and horror only to go have this baby cut from my belly. And certainly not while I was awake! I started pushing against the direction of my nurse, and, thanks to the panic, somehow managed to squeeze my daughter out before the doctor could make it back to my room.

To my surprise—and just to show that there is a higher power somewhere—my daughter came out healthy and beautiful, and I am sure numerous women have written about the moment they first spied their newborns. I think it is indescribable and will leave it to those more poetic than I. Suffice to say, she changed my life forever. That moment gave credibility to all the pregnancy tales I had ever heard and was finding hard to believe. I vowed, *Never again.*

As ecstatic as I was over my new daughter's birth, I soon learned that a baby cannot make a marriage work, another subject I am certain many other authors have tackled, and my marriage was no exception. I filed for divorce and moved out, against the advice of pretty much everyone I knew. I was headstrong and didn't care what anyone thought. I had something inside of me telling me I had to do this. I just wanted to be alone with my daughter and show her that I was willing to do anything for her. She wasn't old enough to understand, but I knew she would be someday.

My husband's parents decided to help him fight for custody of our daughter. She was and is the most important thing in my life, and I was willing to do *anything* to keep her. The thought of losing her, even only part of the time, tore at my insides like nothing I had ever felt. I knew even then that attorneys were expensive, but I vowed to fight for custody to the bitter end—no matter *what* it cost.

I knew I would need a better job to pay my legal fees, but poring over the daily paper proved fruitless. In order to get more pay, I needed to be a manager. In order to be a manager, I needed a degree—no exceptions.

Finally I saw an ad for a stockbroker position and was intrigued. It said that I could make $60,000 the first year, which, in my naïveté, seemed reasonable, and the title of *stockbroker* sounded very professional and exciting. I realize now how ridiculous it all sounds, but I guess my desperation to succeed kept telling me that if anyone could make that kind of money, I could. The icing on the cake was that the ad didn't mention anything about a degree, so I gave them a call.

I secured an interview the next day and skipped work to go to it. The guy interviewing me explained that the job required a bachelor's degree and asked if I had one. Without thinking I said that I did. I didn't realize that in that moment my life had just been changed forever. I had started a ball rolling that wouldn't stop for more than a decade, without even thinking.

As we talked further, I realized that the more I heard about the position, the more I had to have it. I decided to go for it—what was the worst that could happen? Besides, my interviewer, a man, was my age, and I could tell I was the prettiest thing that had stepped into his office in a long time. You could cut the sexual tension with a knife.

I thought back to the day in the basement of that restaurant and decided that if he wanted to be blinded by his dumb stick, then I would allow him to do so. The difference was that I would benefit from it this time. I could tell by his arrogance that he thought he was smarter than I, and somehow that made my use of deception okay.

I filled out an application, on which I stated that I had a bachelor's degree from a school back home, and my interviewer gave me a bunch of paperwork to complete and bring back. The paperwork was a thorough background information questionnaire that would be sent to the SEC, the federal body that governs stockbrokers, which would be reviewed to make sure that I wasn't a criminal. It included previous employers, addresses, names, education, fingerprints, everything. The kicker was that it came with a return envelope that I could seal myself and hand back to my employer to mail to the Feds.

I checked out the SEC Web site and found that although a bachelor's degree was a requirement at the firm I was applying to, it was not a requirement for becoming a licensed stockbroker.

I filled out the questionnaire as accurately as possible and took it back to my employer. I figured if they did check it and asked why I hadn't mentioned my degree, I would simply claim that I must have overlooked the question. That was my first conscious effort to fool an employer. I was aware of what I was doing and made the choice I felt I had to make. This time, I was doing what I felt I had to do to maintain custody of my daughter. It wasn't about appearing better than I was; it was much bigger than that.

They sent the questionnaire off without opening it and hired me shortly thereafter. I worked as a trainee, studying to get my license. Everyone assumed that I was a college graduate, since a bachelor's degree was a minimum requirement at the firm. That presumption of a degree made me an instant Member of the Club, and it felt great. My sister let me borrow some clothes, so I looked the part and I fit in pretty well.

But the job—this wonderful, glamorous, high-powered executive job that I couldn't live without—soon turned out to be a terrible career move with lousy pay and long hours, not at all what I had expected. I could barely pay my rent, put gas in my car, or even feed my daughter, let alone pay my attorney. My once impeccable credit quickly went down the drain. I was struggling to make ends meet and falling farther and farther behind. My desperation grew daily. I realized that I needed a steady paycheck *fast*, before I lost everything.

For several months, I experienced what it was like to be poor. I struggled and didn't know how to cope with my situation. I was making, on average, $400 a month. My rent was $475. I fed my daughter cans of green beans and McDonald's hamburgers (they were 49 cents on Wednesdays) while I went hungry and used change to put gas in my car. If you've never bought 85 cents' worth of gas, let me tell you—it's a humbling experience you won't soon forget. No matter how big a loser the guy behind the counter is, you feel like a bigger one. A cab driver lived next door to me, so when I couldn't afford gas, I would tell him my car broke down (again) and he was nice enough to drive me to work for free. I doubt he believed me, but I could tell he thought I was pretty, so it worked out.

As bad as it got, I never considered financial help from the government. I thought I was "above" that, even though I was a single mother unable to feed her daughter and surely would have qualified for some kind of funding. But I had an image of myself that said, "You're better than that . . . you don't need help from anyone."

I also never considered becoming a stripper or any other questionable occupation that would have tarnished my self-image. I knew people faced with dire circumstances sometimes turned to those things, but it simply wasn't in me. I had to find another way without hurting my daughter, my image, or myself.

But what? I lay awake nights, frightened to death that I would somehow do something to lose custody of my little girl. The thought was so terrifying that I couldn't think of anything else. If push came to shove, I rationalized that I would run away with her. It was ridiculous to think that would work, but I had to have some sort of plan should everything else fail. Somehow I had to learn how to control my fears and succeed as a broker. Selling people thousands of dollars' worth of stocks takes confidence and positive energy. I was lacking in both and failing miserably.

Things had gotten so low for me that, one night, I had just enough change to buy myself a Big Mac. I never particularly liked Big Macs, but it was all I could afford.

After pulling through the drive-through and ordering my sandwich, I grabbed the bag and pulled my car into a parking slot while I unwrapped it. I hadn't eaten for nearly twenty-four hours, and I was so hungry I began to salivate.

I took a big bite and tasted nothing but bread. I spread the buns apart and saw nothing but sauce and lettuce staring back at me. They had forgotten the meat. I started to cry right there in the parking lot and cried all the way home. I never felt lower. I know now that there are people who suffer through worse things every day, but you couldn't have convinced me of it then. I felt like screaming, but I couldn't even manage that.

I ate the rest of my "burger" because I was too hungry to throw it away. Somehow, the meal only made me feel worse. Chewing up every morsel and swallowing it made me feel like a failure. I couldn't even take it back and get a new one because I was crying and too embarrassed to show my poor, downtrodden face in public.

Life sure wasn't turning out the way I had planned. I couldn't seem to find the short road around anything anymore. I was faced with having to tackle my issues head-on. I no longer felt like the exception to the rule. Maybe, I began to think, I was never meant to skate through life without a worry in the world and loaded with dough. Maybe I was just as vulnerable as everyone else. That thought was startling.

As the days passed, I felt more and more like a failure. I had no real friends, and, to make matters worse, my sister was gradually turning against me. At least that's how it felt. She was sure that I had made a mistake by getting divorced. She thought I should have stayed married and become a housewife so I could stay home with my baby.

By then, she was remarried and didn't have to work, so it was easy for her to pass judgment on someone less fortunate. She seemed to forget that she had been divorced not that long ago. She seemed to forget that people need to work in order to pay their bills. I felt as if she was daring me to come up with another solution.

But I knew I couldn't stay with someone I couldn't even stand to look at. I couldn't understand any suggestion to the contrary. The only thing for me to do was to cut her out of my life. I couldn't take any more negative energy and I couldn't bear to wonder if I had acted rashly. Besides, it was too late for those kinds of thoughts. They would only breed self-doubt and worry. I needed something positive to focus on until I could discover a way out of the dark.

Enter my next boyfriend.

The vice president of the brokerage firm took an interest in me, and I began spending time outside of work with him. He was recently divorced and fifteen years my senior, but he was good looking, wealthy, and kind. He paid my phone bills, since he lived out west most of the time and we talked on the phone a lot. When he was in town, he bought me food and supplies for my daughter. He never knew how poor I really was, because I was an expert at hiding things like that, but I think he sensed that I needed a little help and dug right in. I was too proud to ask for anything more, even though I am sure he would have given it to me. He was a pleasure to spend time with and I respected him as a businessman.

He gave me a lot of good advice for work and taught me about self-affirmation and self-worth in ways I hadn't thought about before. I learned how to appear strong in the face of adversity, even if I wasn't feeling it. He taught me to see the glass half full and gave me lessons on how to consciously change my perspective. I suppose all that amounted to was yet another lesson in faking it until I made it. But he gave me hope for the future when I was at my lowest.

Part of my new guy's job at the firm was motivating the brokers to feel empowered so that they in turn could sell more stocks, and his motivational speeches spilled over into his personal life. He was great at giving pep talks and always left me feeling fantastic about myself. If I was down, he gave me a few words of encouragement, and his positive influence on me proved critical during one of the bleakest times of my life.

We eventually decided to part ways because we lived so far apart, but during the short time we were together, I learned a lot about forging ahead and putting a positive spin on things. I was still broke, but I was a little more sure of myself and able to see through the cloud of fear and doubt that had surrounded my life. I learned how to tell myself I could make it through each day by containing all that negative energy that had built up inside me.

Shortly after we had ended our relationship, I managed to snag a personal meeting with a big fish of a client. I felt that he could be my chance to finally begin making some money. The client insisted on meeting in person, which was status quo for the really big ones, and I scrambled to make myself appear to be the person I had portrayed myself to be over the phone—Miss Huge Stockbroker. I went to one of the head brokers in my firm and asked a favor: I asked if I could take one of his cars to the meeting. My own car wasn't exactly a rust bucket, but it wasn't a stunner by any means. I knew he had lots of cars, some actually awarded to him for being such a great broker, and I figured he wouldn't mind sharing the wealth.

To my surprise, he began lecturing me on what he thought my problem was. He told me it didn't matter what kind of car I drove or what clothes I wore; it mattered how I came across during the meeting. I had to physically stop myself from rolling my eyes at all that garbage talk. I couldn't believe my ears—this, coming from the superbroker who wouldn't be caught dead without his $4,000 monkey suit, suspenders, and $500 shoes. He would have been reduced to nothing had he been faced with pulling up to meet a client in a piece-of-crap Buick. It's just like the person who has an office and yet swears he could do the same job from a cubicle. Easy to say from the top.

I ended up taking my own car to the meeting and wearing the best suit I had. I tripped and fell going into the restaurant where we had agreed to meet and never did end up landing the account.

To this day I think that broker's advice was crap. I would have been much more sure of myself had I had the right car and outfit in which to present myself. First impressions mean everything to most people, and that is especially true for someone who will be handling their finances.

If I had spoken to someone on the phone and decided to meet him to see what he could do with my million dollars and he pulled up in a $9,000 Buick wearing clothes that didn't fit right, I would have given him exactly what I got that day—*nothing*. People who tell you that wealth doesn't matter or appearances are futile have never had to worry about such things. They preach their garbage from behind their fancy desks, in their fancy clothes, and they derive power from telling you that physical trappings don't mean a thing. I would have loved to have been able to believe in those types of high ideals, but I didn't have much more time to remain poor. The bottom line was that in my haphazardly chosen career I was expected to maintain a certain image that I couldn't possibly maintain using my weekly paycheck. The clients would see through it, even if they couldn't hear through it on the phone.

With every failure came more confusion and desperation. I had never failed at anything before, and I hated it. I feared that my life was beginning to outpace my high school skill set. It's a horrible feeling to wonder for the first time in your life if maybe you aren't smarter than everyone else, after all.

Desperate for funds, I visited one of those places that loan you money in exchange for your car title. My car was a piece of crap, but I didn't owe any money on it at the time, so I was able to borrow a couple thousand dollars and buy myself some time. Unfortunately, I soon realized that a car title loan payment at a million and a half percent interest was going to break me very quickly. I decided at that point I had no choice but to keep faking it until I made it. It was time to change jobs, and I didn't have time to dillydally around with anything except higher-paying management positions. I made the decision to "fudge" my résumé a little bit more and start shopping around for the position I felt I needed, if not deserved.

I worked up a new vitae with a made-up degree printed in bold under the education section and put my GPA as 3.2. Why not? That's probably what I would have gotten had I gone to college, right? I really had that thought on that day, as strange as it might sound. It was as if I had to make my fake persona match my real one—or the one I would have had if I'd ever had the chance to develop it.

I also knew that things that appeared too good to be true usually weren't, and I didn't want to raise any red flags by applying for an entry-level management position with a cum laude from Harvard, so I left out all references to my being a CPA, since I had learned just how easily that could be checked from my prior experience with my first husband. At least I had taken *something* away from that marriage. Good God.

I began sending my résumé out and calling on companies that were looking to fill management positions. Finally, I got a call back for an interview. I was very nervous. I kept thinking they were going to put me in a room to tell me they had checked my background and I didn't have a degree. Or maybe they would ask me some top-secret question that only college graduates were told the answer to and flush me out right then and there. I would have to sit there like a big dummy with egg on my face while they all looked on in disgust. It was all I could think about.

Oddly enough, on the day of the big interview, the question of my degree—this major portion of my fabricated life—never once entered the conversation. It just sat there, several big, bold marks on a piece of paper, doing nothing. I did all the talking and must have done a good job. They offered me the position on the spot for $37,000 a year. That was about $33,000 more than I was making as a stockbroker, and I didn't waste much time in accepting. My new title was *business manager* and I would be handling the company's 401(k) plan and accounting staff. I even got a thousand-dollar sign-on bonus. Things couldn't have looked brighter, and it suddenly dawned on me: This college education stuff was even better than I had thought it would be!

My first day on the job, I took a basic skills test, debit and credit stuff. I failed miserably, much to the surprise of my new boss. The look on his face was pained, and I knew I had to say something fast. I laughed and said that it had been so long since I had done accounting by hand that I had reversed the debits/credits—*hahaha*—and that I was there to take their bookkeeping into the twenty-first century, remember? We had a chuckle over that and swept the entire unfortunate hiccup under the rug. Neither one of us knew what else to do, so we simply forged ahead with our mutual choices.

But later that evening, I purchased an old college accounting textbook and brushed up on debits and credits. It didn't take long or cost much.

Once again I had found the short road. And nobody, I was convinced, had gotten hurt.

# CHAPTER FIVE

My new boss ended up being my first real mentor, and I realized I had learned more from people like him than I *ever* could have learned in school. Of course I had no baseline to compare it to, but when has that ever stopped me?

My boss taught me how to manage people and how to play office politics while remaining the consummate professional. I was like a giant sponge and wanted nothing more than to be just like him. I mimicked his style of management and did whatever he said. I was never pretentious. If anything, I was too down-to-earth—too real—in order to compensate for what only I knew lived deep down inside.

I never exhibited the huge ego that some college grads have, so I had no bad habits or unrealistic expectations of what my job should be. I didn't mind working hard or doing the grunt work. I never complained because I was thrilled just to be there. My boss saw himself in me and began to trust more in my abilities every day. He was the firm's CFO, and he was slowly phasing himself into retirement. He was up-front about my being too "green" to take over as CFO when he was gone, but he said that I had room to grow under whomever they hired to take his place.

He forced me into public-speaking situations and had me take his place at important meetings that to him had become a bore but to me were still exciting. My yearly review was always off-the-record, and he gave me very specific and invaluable advice. He told me that my voice was too quiet, my hair was too blonde, and my skirts were too short. I took his directions seriously, changed my image, and soon gained more respect as a manager and colleague.

Under his guidance, I learned that people doubt those who don't seem to be who they're supposed to be. I was every inch what a college graduate should be and, so far as I know, no one ever doubted it. Well . . . except perhaps one person.

I worked closely with a lady in my department who, I could tell from the beginning, wasn't crazy about me. She had been with the firm since I was in diapers, and she thought I was a young whippersnapper of the worst kind. She didn't have a degree and was stuck in her position forever. Until I arrived on the scene, she had compensated for her educational liability by being the boss's right hand, but now I was the showstopper.

I understood what she was feeling but I was helpless to stop it. I tried to make friends with her, but it was a long road. She was nice enough to me but very reserved, and my radar was telling me she would stab me in the back at the first opportunity. I knew this was someone to be very watchful of and treated her with the utmost respect, even when she wasn't there personally.

I also knew that she had access to my personnel file, which made me nervous. But, as time passed and she stopped viewing me as a threat to her very existence, she warmed up to me. One afternoon, as we chatted about various things, she told me a story about someone she used to work with. The story went like this: She had already been with the firm for years and some new girl got hired for the department. The girl said that she had a college degree. The woman said that she didn't believe the girl for some reason and knew the company didn't do a background check, so she decided to check for herself. She said she found out that sure enough the girl *didn't* have a degree.

I couldn't believe my ears. Was she trying to tell me something? I'm sure I was squirming in my chair. The woman continued her story as if she hadn't noticed until I heard myself squeak out the question: "What did you do?" She said she told the boss and the new girl left.

She never batted an eye at my apparent stress, and I gained an entirely new respect for her that day.

I knew she had found me out, but I also knew she wasn't going to tell. She could have sold me down the river whenever she wanted, but for some reason she never did. I may never know why, but I hope that it was because I had gained her respect and she saw that I wasn't really a bad person. Maybe she just figured I was the best she could hope for from the pool of egomaniacs out there. She had been around a long time and was smart enough to recognize the lesser of two evils. Maybe she saw that I worked hard and overcompensated for my shortcomings rather than expecting things to be handed to me, or maybe she just liked the idea of having something on me that she could drop like a bomb whenever she chose, should I ever cross her.

It was an eye-opening experience.

During my next four years with the firm I was privy to numerous private upper-management conversations regarding the underedu-cated masses in the company. I got to hear what the graduates really thought of the nongraduates. I was the fly on the wall and got to see firsthand what people would have said about me had they known who I really was. I belonged to groups within the firm to which only the higher educated were allowed to belong.

During one meeting in particular, the discussion referenced the problem of retaining good employees and what the requirements should be for some of the lower-level production staff. By that they meant people with two-year degrees, and everyone agreed those people must have been a little lazier and less motivated than those with full-fledged bachelor's degrees—never mind those with no degree at all, whom they simply referred to as "monkeys chained to computers."

Those were the words from the president of the firm, and they made me realize why they couldn't retain these employees—they had no respect for anyone who wasn't like them. In fact, they saw themselves so far removed from the masses of undereducated employees that they couldn't even piece together what their interests might be.

So there I sat, unchained from my computer, at least for the time being, chuckling with the club about how we could possibly plant a banana tree in the lobby, and pretending that was the funniest thing I had heard all day. In reality, I felt sick to my stomach and wanted nothing more than to climb up on the table and start swinging my arms below my knees, making orangutan noises. I opted against it, because they probably only would have laughed louder.

As the days came and passed, I found myself working harder than most of the other managers, probably a form of compensation to keep anyone who may have doubted my qualifications at arm's length. My salary increased substantially quite quickly. Everything was going well. And then the day came when it was time for me to fire someone.

Not just any someone, either, but a friend of mine. She worked in my department, and we had hung out with different groups of people now and then after work. She looked up to me and was a relatively good employee. She had recently broken up with her longtime boyfriend, and she was constantly taking personal phone calls. It wasn't long before my boss noticed. The firm was struggling a bit financially, and the president decided to cut staff wherever possible. Out of ten or so people in accounting, we had to send one packing. Since my friend was the most junior employee, it soon became obvious that her days were numbered.

My boss informed me of the decision and at the same time told me I would be performing the layoff. I knew a few days in advance, and I don't think I slept until after it was over. She was young and unmarried, with no kids, and would recover quickly. None of that seemed to matter. I was very upset by what lay ahead.

The day came and my boss checked in on me. He saw how upset I was and agreed at least to be in the room with me when it happened. I knew he thought this was important for me to do, and I knew he was right. This was something a manager *had* to do.

We called her into my office, and although I am entirely sure she had no idea before that moment, I saw the realization on her face. I started into my speech about the firm and the cutbacks and she began to cry. I felt so bad for her. She begged to keep her job and asked if there was *anything* she could do. I looked to my boss and he took over from there, explaining that she would get two weeks' severance pay and a reference letter.

To this day, I have never experienced what she went through that day, but I would venture to say that my own pain from the opposite side of the desk matched hers. I wanted to stand up and tell her to forget it and then give her my job. But business doesn't work that way. That was her last day at the firm, and nothing was going to change that.

She called my home number a few times after that, but I never answered. I was afraid she would beg me like she did that day and I couldn't bear the thought of that. I learned that socializing with people who worked for me should be done with care and purpose, not to make friends. Although firing her was beyond my control, I'm sure she still felt as if I had let her down, even though I was only doing my job.

With that trauma in my past, life began looking up again . . . even more so, I felt, when I met the man who would eventually become my second husband. He worked at the firm, too, but not as a manager. He didn't have a bachelor's degree either, but I decided not to tell him my secret. I knew that was the wrong thing to do, but I cannot express enough how much of my life revolved around my ability to pay my attorney. I felt as if I couldn't risk telling the new man in my life what I had done and have him spill the beans. I rationalized my deceit by

61

telling myself it would be a burden on him if I told him. I would be asking him to compromise his morals, and that wouldn't be fair. I knew if he asked me to come clean to the world I would have to say no and lose him forever, and that simply wasn't worth the risk.

I was on the short road, for better or worse, and I wasn't about to derail myself just because I was going to get married. I told myself I lied to him to protect him, but to be honest, I lied to protect myself. I realize how bad that sounds, but my inner voice told me I was doing the right thing.

To his credit, I don't think he would have judged me. In fact, since he also lacked a degree, maybe it would have been a relief to him to learn the truth. Maybe he would have thought it was funny how I had bucked the system. Still, there was always a small part of me that wondered if he would ever see me in the same light again. After all, here he was dating the business manager of the firm he worked for—a hero among the monkeys, no doubt. What would he think if he found out I was something much less than that? Would he want to marry someone whose healthy income hinged on a background check? Maybe he was in love with the hotshot image I portrayed. Maybe that was what had attracted him to me in the first place. If that were the case, I would be a fool to tell him.

So I entered into the marriage with the skeleton still hanging in my closet. I never gave him the chance to show me what he was made of. I couldn't trust in that. I couldn't trust in anything because I was a liar myself. I couldn't believe anyone would want the real me. I was too afraid to peek out from behind the disguise and reveal the real me, not even to him. He loved me, and I knew that, but in my heart I had to keep that love at arm's length because that, too, could be lost.

I added my marriage to the list of important things I could lose if my secret were ever discovered. If he didn't leave me after the humiliation, then surely he would leave me for lying to him. He would feel as if he were a fool to have believed in me. He would feel no different than my pregnant friend whose husband was a snake. He would feel he didn't know me at all. The saddest part is that he would have been right. I struggled internally with my decision, but I decided the battle was one I had to wage alone.

In turn, my new husband completed the image of myself I had conjured up. He didn't know *me*, but he loved me—albeit the puppet me, the fake and phony and fraud. He's a good man who, like me, enjoys the finer things in life, and over the years I made sure he had every toy a grown man could want. I gave him everything I thought he needed. He had come from humble beginnings and never ceased to be amazed at anything shiny and new. He enjoyed his newfound bragging rights and never had to worry about waking up one day to find everything was gone. I always worried that he might take to heart the adage "If it seems to good to be true, then it probably is" and figure me out. He climbed aboard the ride during its first big upswing, and I made sure he enjoyed all the fruits of financial freedom. I envied his unawareness of all the risk. I would have given anything for one day of reprieve from the worry that plagued me daily in my own little world.

I look back now and wish I had simply blurted it out: "Hey, I'm not really who you think I am!" I wish I had just told him and let the cards fall wherever they might. But I didn't. I didn't, and therefore I never felt he knew me in those days. I eventually reached a point in my development where I did reveal my lie to him, but in the meantime I lost a critical opportunity to be loved for who I was instead of wondering if I was loved only for the person I pretended to be. I tricked someone who loved me, someone who married me. I let myself be a phony and I let him believe I was that person. My husband married an inflated version of his wife and had no idea who I really was for the first four years of our marriage. I did all that based on what I thought was good for him. Or maybe that is giving myself too much credit. I needed him to complete my phony image, not only in my mind's eye, but also in the eyes of the court. I consciously deceived him.

I don't mean to make it sound as if it were planned or contrived that way, because it wasn't. I thought he was handsome and kind and sweet. I knew he loved me early on and my inability to love myself made that feel wonderful. I had moments of doubt because I knew he didn't *really* know me, but otherwise I enjoyed spending time with him and knew he was someone who was meant to be part of my life. My emotional being was so extremely shallow at that point that I didn't know what love was or what form it should take. I only had my limited, two-dimensional image of myself in my mind, and he fit into the image perfectly. He was the ideal husband, and that was just what I needed.

# CHAPTER SIX

I was finally making enough money to pay my attorney, and, with my husband's help, I was able to gain full custody of my daughter. I felt as if I had been through a war, but it was finally over. The prior two years had been a huge struggle, with so many custody hearings and evaluations and with everything I did under a microscope. In the end, I believe that my getting married to a stable guy is what really turned everything in my favor. I hadn't changed, of course, but I had in the court's eyes. Even the court system was more interested in images than in actual facts.

Although the decision that day had been in my favor, I came out of the battle having lost a lot of faith in the judicial system. I had been through so many unfair meetings and listened to so many people lie about my daughter and me out of spite or vengeance that I had a hard time understanding what any of it had to do with justice. I watched as the judge seemed irritated even to be there, and I watched the attorneys battle it out for their egos and their pocketbooks more than for their clients. I saw that no one would be totally happy in the end, but there was no way to stop the destruction. I felt powerless and out of control, and I hated that feeling. It wasn't about what was real, it was about what was *perceived* to be real, and the person with the most money and the nicest place to live could sway everyone's perception.

In the end that person turned out to be me, but what kind of a lesson did we all take away from it? I wasn't a bad person, but neither was my ex-husband—and yet there we were, tearing each other apart through our lawyers and saying so many things that could never be taken back.

I think the best advice I got during that time was from my two-year-old daughter. We were driving down a quiet road one day when we spotted an old lady walking down the sidewalk wearing a large goofy-looking hat. My daughter asked me, "Why is that lady wearing that hat?" and I replied, "I don't know." She looked at me with a puzzled expression and I told her, "I don't know everything."

She replied, "I know everything." I asked, "Oh yeah? And what do you know?" She looked me in the eye and said, very matter-of-factly, "People are just people, and oranges make you poop."

I had to admit that she had an excellent point, and that tidbit got me through more hard days than I care to remember.

I got the news from my attorney that I had been awarded custody while on vacation in North Carolina with my husband, my daughter, and my parents. My husband and I were just pulling into the driveway of our rented home when my cell phone rang. I recognized my attorney's number on the caller ID, and I knew he had no other reason for calling other than to tell me that some sort of decision had been made. My palms began to sweat, but I answered, and he told me that my ex-husband was ready to end his fight if I would agree to a lesser amount of monthly child support than state guidelines mandated. I couldn't believe that it had—once again—come down to money. I didn't care about the money—especially not now that I was doing so well financially—and jumped at the offer. Now I could finally quit worrying and begin taking back control of my life from the courts.

And then the most unexpected of things happened. I was finally able to accept the depth of my love for my daughter. It's almost as if I had been holding back in a way because I was so terrified of what losing custody of her would have done to me. The darkness of my life would have been unimaginable, and for the two years it took to battle it out I kept my emotions at bay. It was as if I was afraid to face the feelings because I was afraid that they would force me to see the "what if?" side of things, and that would have sent me over the edge. Or, at any rate, to Mexico.

So I was finally able to accept the capacity of the feelings I had for her and could embrace them, comfortable at last in the notion that she meant everything to me—more so, as it turned out, than life itself.

Now, finally, I could put thoughts of Plan B safely out of my head forever. It was as if someone had stuck me in the microwave on quick defrost. I hugged my daughter every five minutes for days on end. I cried a lot that week—it was a fantastic vacation.

# CHAPTER SEVEN

With my custody battle over and my major financial woes behind me, I entered a new and frightening era in my life. My justification for living a lie was over. I no longer had to fight for money to hire an attorney to fight for custody of the person I loved the most. Now all I had to figure out was what exactly I was doing and my reasons for doing it. Suddenly, I no longer had to lie to survive. Now I had a choice in the matter . . . a chance to do the *right* thing.

And then one day, while reading something in a magazine or newspaper, I came across an interesting concept that I hadn't thought about before: *victimless crime*. In essence, a victimless crime is a crime that doesn't harm anyone or anything.

I thought that was an intriguing notion. Until then, I had always assumed that all crimes hurt somebody. But maybe I'd been wrong. Maybe my lie fell into this category. Offhand, I couldn't name anyone I had victimized by working under false pretenses. Except maybe— and it's a stretch for sure—some other nameless person who would have gotten my job if I hadn't come along.

I thought about other crimes that some people perceive to fall into this category—prostitution, suicide, and gambling. Even these all seemed to have victims, even if the victim was only the person committing the act. But I wasn't a victim—I hadn't prostituted myself or slit my wrists or squandered all my money at the casino. I really did seem to be committing a truly victimless crime.

I mean, I benefited financially, which might appear to be selfish, but so did my daughter and my husband and everyone I helped at work. I was doing a great job, getting my work done, and making people's lives easier and more rewarding every day. I wasn't stealing anything or hurting anyone. I was earning my paycheck each week and was otherwise living a very moral life. I was sort of like Robin Hood without the armed robbery, a hero for the undereducated. Maybe that is a bit of a stretch, but, then again, maybe it's not, especially not if you ask the monkeys. Life doesn't have a rewind button, and I suddenly couldn't see any reason to pull the plug on something that was going so well. The question of right and wrong became one of convenience and compromise. If it ain't broke . . .

So, after paying down some of our accumulated debts, my family and I were able to start enjoying our income. It felt great to have money left over between paychecks after paying for all the necessities. We spent most of our extra cash on our house and spared no expense on furnishings. I loved decorating the place, and just sitting in the living room and looking around at everything we *owned* made me feel terrific. Here was concrete evidence that we were successful. The proof was all around us.

We began throwing parties for every occasion we could come up with. We wanted to show off all the things we had accumulated, since that made our possessions feel all the more satisfying. We spent $10,000 building an addition onto our house, which we turned into a bar. We threw stock-the-bar parties and invited all of the people we felt were just like us—young, successful, and popular. I made food and the alcohol flowed. Our parties lasted into the wee hours of the night, and everyone looked forward to them. I enjoyed being the hostess because it made me feel so grown up. It also gave me the illusion of having a lot of friends.

The people who came were mostly my husband's friends, but they had wives or girlfriends, too, so—*voila!*—I had "friends." We all sat around and bragged about ourselves or bet money on poker and darts. People dressed up or wore costumes or came in whatever gear the sports season warranted. We made furnishing and decorating decisions based on our party plans. We rented snow machines and disco lights and decorated for every holiday that existed—and a few that didn't. We wanted to show everyone how far we had come, and we did it in grand style.

I sailed through the next few years having a pretty good time. But then I hit a spell of bad luck toward the end of my tenure at the firm. I got into a car accident midyear and ended up with a leg injury that causes me pain to this day. I also suffered a head injury that required fifteen stitches. I had no sooner recovered from that when I had to have emergency surgery as a result of a ruptured ovarian cyst. That put me out of commission for a while, but something good came of it all. My sister came to the hospital to visit me, and we renewed our friendship. We hadn't spoken since my custody battle and it felt good to bury the last remaining ill blood from those difficult times so very long ago.

As a child, I had never been one who was always getting hurt, so my medical setbacks were scary for me. They made me realize that I wasn't invincible after all. I realized that I had a physical body that had to remain healthy or else I could lose everything. I had never stopped to think about that before. I had never been what you'd call a thrill seeker, but I had ridden a few roller coasters and whatnot in my younger days. After that bout of bad luck, I began thinking a little more cautiously about my activities.

Getting hurt took valuable time away from my pursuit of happiness. I had been on pain medication for months, and my work suffered because of it. There were days during that time when I thought I was being punished for compromising my moral values. I kept those thoughts locked deep inside me because they seemed crazy. Lying in bed for days was obviously doing me no good—too much time to think things through and to allow the paranoia to creep back into my life. I would simply have to fight to keep it under control.

Something else I realized I would have to fight was going to prove an even tougher foe. While I'd been convalescing, I gained fifty pounds. I had never had a weight problem before. As a teenager I could eat a whole pizza and still weigh a hundred pounds soaking wet. I gained thirty-six pounds during pregnancy, of which twenty-six disappeared at birth. The other ten melted off within weeks without any problem.

The weirdest part about gaining so much weight so quickly was that I didn't even know it. I didn't own a scale, and somehow I justified the increase in my clothing size from 6 to 14 as some sort of fluke—maybe the sizes of more expensive clothes run small. Not until I saw a picture of myself did I come to the shocking realization that I had become a tub-o-lard. It was a photo of me standing in my driveway, and I literally didn't recognize myself. I had to ask my husband who the person in the picture was, and he thought I was kidding. I was stunned to find out it was me.

At first I couldn't look away from the picture. It was like a car wreck that's so awful you just can't stop staring. The next day, I ran out and bought a scale. I was stunned at what I saw.

I don't know how to explain what it feels like to go to bed thin and wake up fat. The day before I had an image in my mind of what I looked like. I looked in the mirror every day and never saw it coming. Then I saw that picture, and *bam!*—I was overweight. I was embarrassed. I was shocked. I couldn't believe I had been walking around wearing skirts and heels and driving my convertible and all the while people must have been looking at me wondering what I was thinking. My self-image—that thing that I had worked so hard to perfect—was all mucked up.

I have heard about a phenomenon called distorted body image, which is present in some cases of bulimia and anorexia. It's when a person can look in the mirror and, no matter how thin he or she is, see a fat person looking back. I believe I was suffering from this, except in reverse. I could look in the mirror and like what I saw, even though in real life I was overweight. The concept scared and fascinated me at the same time. Even after I had weighed myself, I still didn't see the fat person in the mirror. I mean, sure, I wasn't trying on bathing suits or anything, but my body didn't look that different in the reflection. I didn't see any lumps or rolls or cellulite, so where the heck were the fifty pounds I could clearly see in the picture? I grabbed the picture and held it up next to my reflection, and the two looked completely different to me. Was I hallucinating? I didn't think so, and surely the scale was correct.

Had my being a phony every day of my life actually spilled over into not recognizing the real physical me I had become? I wondered if my brain was so focused on this image of the person I was expected to be that even my mind couldn't differentiate what was real from what wasn't. Or worse yet, perhaps I was mentally ill and needed therapy. I was terrified that my eyes seemed to be playing tricks on me, even when I knew what I should be seeing. Maybe I had become one of those people who walk around thinking they're Jesus without realizing everyone else knows they're not. Maybe I was some crazy nut who thought everyone admired me, when in fact everyone was merely pitying me and I was too far gone to know the difference. I stared at my reflection and the picture for another few minutes and decided I must be a little crazy, but I also realized that this weight thing was a definite problem, and it definitely had to be addressed.

Over the next several months I shut down as a woman. My self-confidence had taken a blow, and I no longer felt pretty or sexy or anything a woman in her twenties should feel. I beat myself up inside trying to figure out how I had got to that point without noticing. I no longer looked in the mirror, since it seemed to be a waste of time. I dyed my hair darker—the color of mud—and began buying pants instead of skirts. Rarely did I wear makeup, and for the first time in my life I felt the term frumpy applied to me.

I didn't want to be touched or looked at and wore sweat pants and baggy T-shirts when I was home. I felt as if everywhere I went people were staring at me and feeling sorry for me. It was ridiculous—I know that now—but at the time I was so self-centered that I couldn't see past my own nose. At times I thought I could actually feel myself jiggling in all the wrong places when I walked. My weight gain became the excuse for anything that had gone wrong for me throughout the past six months. I blamed everyone I knew for not telling me. I was determined to correct the problem as soon as possible.

It was during this time that I acquired the nickname "Ice Princess" from my husband. I am certain that the sudden discovery of my weight gain resulted in a sudden freeze of everything sweet I had ever been. I no longer liked to be looked at or touched. I had never been a touchy-feely person, but I became a gross exaggeration of that. Kisses were allowed only on the cheek, definitely no tongue, and lights-on romance became a thing of the past. I was reeling from my discovery, and my husband couldn't understand it. I felt disgusting and resented him for not pointing my weight out to me. I got angry thinking that he was faking his attraction for me and couldn't possibly understand why he would want to touch me. I was angry and confused, and I began to turn off my emotions. I was shutting down.

I had no idea that I had based so much of my self-worth and physical image on being sexy. If I wasn't sexy, then how was I attracting my husband? It didn't make sense and I couldn't stand the dichotomy. My husband had always told me that he loved me, but I began to twist it around and say he just wanted something from me.

I felt as if I couldn't figure out how to fix that part of my life, so I had to fix the underlying problem. I had to shed the pounds and be the beautiful wife I used to think I was. I thought of it as a role, which was ridiculous. But until I could get back to the image I had in my head, all affection was irritating. The best way I can explain it is that I wanted him to want to sleep with me because I was sexy, not because he was horny. If I didn't feel I looked sexy, then I couldn't believe he thought I was—so that left the latter as his only possible motivation. That made my blood run cold.

I think I was so two-dimensional at that point in my life that I couldn't understand love or what it meant. I didn't understand he was looking for love in the form of affection. I didn't understand that love can exist even when people don't feel they look right. I was so focused on my image that I couldn't see past what I thought everything was supposed to look like on the surface. I thought since I looked different things must have changed. I was extremely shallow, and it is no wonder my new nickname stuck.

Over the years, I had learned that when one piece of life doesn't make sense, we tend to focus on the pieces that do. I think it's a survival mechanism. It helped me feel in control to go to work and have people respond to me for my work or abilities, but at home I couldn't make sense of why my husband responded at all. I know it sounds shallow, but I withdrew physically and emotionally, and I am sure our relationship suffered. I threw myself into my work, and he, into his hobbies. He loved me anyway, and I hoped he understood I was going through something terrible inside. I felt very alone most of the time but could not explain the depth of my self-doubt. We would joke about the Ice Princess from time to time, but it was never really that funny.

I joined Weight Watchers and started my road to weight loss. I was nothing if not dedicated. I called my mom and demanded to know why she hadn't mentioned my weight to me when she had seen me at Thanksgiving. She sounded surprised and, like my husband, thought I was kidding. I have since destroyed all photos of myself during that period of my life. Looking at them was disturbing, not so much for the oddness of seeing myself like that but for the sense of not being aware of something so obvious—something I could see and feel and had been able to deny until faced with photographic evidence. Was I delusional? Could I possibly be that unaware of how I looked? What *else* had I missed? I became paranoid that everything wasn't as it had seemed. I needed to prove to myself that I was living the life I thought I was.

I can only guess that since I had never struggled with my weight in the past, I wasn't on the lookout for it. Besides, the guys at the 7-Eleven never stopped hooting and hollering, so how bad could it be? Then I remembered the clowns who had tried to buy me hot chocolate at the bar when I was pregnant and realized that men will hit on women no matter what. They didn't care that I was fifty pounds over-weight; in fact, it probably made my clothes a little tighter, and that was never a drawback. Now every time I looked in the mirror I was disgusted and anxious. I looked at my hands and could swear my fingers looked like sausages. How could I have not known?

But as with most things in my life, even this negative became a positive. I see now that being overweight was actually good for my career. Before I realized that I was fat, I used to sashay into every meeting thinking I was one hot corporate mamma in my styling suits. I had the confidence of a size 6, albeit the brains and body of a size 14. What that created for me was the triple whammy: (1) men who were my superiors were older than I and therefore didn't mind the extra fifty pounds; (2) women didn't view me as a threat or an airhead; and (3) I was completely clueless and therefore the most confident big girl you'd ever want to meet. I can say with 100 percent certainty that I would have never been hired at my next position had I not been overweight. I had begun my weight loss regimen, and I was losing weight, but not quickly enough to suit me.

# CHAPTER EIGHT

There I was, getting away with it, life on track, making money, being a corporate manager—and yet somehow still not satisfied. My relationship with my boss eventually soured because he didn't approve of my relationship with my husband. Not that he cared that I was married to someone at work; I think it had more to do with the fact my husband wasn't a manager. Maybe he thought I would tell all their engineering secrets in the throes of passion? Can you imagine? "Oh yes baby, YES! Some layoffs are happening next month!" Or maybe when you're part of the club, you aren't supposed to breed outside the line? Those half-monkey, half-educated humanoid kids can be pretty funny looking.

My unhappiness at work was growing daily, but I had my husband's support, which kept me going. Still, in time I began to feel that I needed to take a chance and jump ship. I sent my still-inflated résumé to several firms, all the while hearing the voice in my head warning me that this was a bad idea. I was aware that background checks were becoming more common, but I also knew that such checks were an expensive endeavor and that not every company had a real system in place yet.

I knew I probably wouldn't be lucky enough to stumble onto another firm that simply didn't have a human resources department, but maybe—just maybe—I could find one without a system or a system with loopholes that I could take advantage of. Some companies still had Suzie Secretary making the calls, and certainly I could hope for Suzie to be having a lazy day. I am nothing, after all, if not the eternal optimist.

I interviewed at three companies worth writing about, the first being a marketing firm in St. Petersburg. They loved everything about me, and the interview ended with them telling me they would be putting an offer together shortly. I could almost see them drool. The position sounded perfect for me. The company was young minded, with a fun atmosphere. They saw in me a very together, well-spoken, hard-working twenty-something with a track record of getting the job done. Oh, and a college grad. I almost forgot.

Then the bad news came. I had to sign a release form for a background check—normally not a deal breaker, except this one was quite specific and definitely indicated that these people had a real *system*. The form listed the name of the third-party company that would be doing the search as well as exactly what they would be checking and how they would be checking it. They were paying someone else to make sure the check got done. Education was at the top of their list. They called with a fabulous offer and I promptly declined, much to their surprise. Easy come, easy go, I suppose—but all because of that damned degree. I still felt cheated.

The next offer I received was from another engineering firm, and also from the biggest jerk I have ever met on an interview. He was the very fat and sweaty CFO of his firm, and in his self-absorbed, bloated opinion, that made him better than everyone else. The man looked as if he was about to pop as he sat across the table from me. He was bright red in color and I am certain his blood pressure was off the charts, considering how tightly wound the man was.

He swore approximately ten times in the first ten minutes and proceeded to discuss his secretary's poor mental health while she sat there listening, eyes down, as if she had been instructed not to look at me. A self-proclaimed "asshole," he was looking for someone to run the accounting department there because he was needed in Texas. He requested that I come back for a second interview.

I don't know what possessed me to go back, but I did. I think I wanted to try to somehow save his employees from this wretched man. Upon my arrival I was asked to complete some paperwork. And, sure enough, there it was—the waiver for a background check. It was simple and obviously concocted in-house, so I hoped for the Lazy Suzie scenario, signed the form, and went in to meet with Mr. Sweaty for the second time.

After more swearing and lots of bragging, his mentally ill secretary came in and handed him a note. He looked at the note, looked at me, and cut the interview short, saying he had to attend to something right away. Could it be that she had been making the background check calls during my interview? My heart was pounding and I wanted to make my exit as quickly as possible. I am certain I could have rivaled his blood pressure point-for-point at that moment.

We shook hands, and I made a beeline for the elevator. I thought that would be the last I would hear from that company, but Mr. Sweaty called a week later and offered me a position with a nice salary. Needless to say I was surprised, but I declined his offer via telephone, and he actually hung up on me before I could tell him why. Besides wanting to hang onto what was left of my *own* mental health, the truth was that I had already received a better offer.

The interview for the position I ended up taking was with yet another engineering firm in town. It was for an accounting manager position, working for the biggest bitch in the industry.

The engineering world is quite small, and everyone knows everyone, so I had actually heard about the woman with whom I interviewed long before I met her. We had our first interview in her office, a fifteen-by-fifteen-foot corner office with nothing in it except a desk and a file cabinet. The only picture was a self-portrait, a glamour shot of sorts—rather narcissistic, I thought, for this woman who in real life did not appear even to wear makeup. She was overweight, and as I mentioned earlier, I am certain we seemed kindred on that front. If I had been blonde and a size 6 at the time, the interview would have ended after about five minutes. She was a no-nonsense type who appreciated others who appeared to be the same. Luckily for me, I could appear to be whatever it was that she hoped I'd be.

She talked about herself and all of her possessions for an hour, while I sat there and smiled like an idiot. To my surprise, she came across as very nice, and I noticed there was no degree hanging on her wall. I wondered about that, but did not ask.

She said that I would have to have another interview with several other managers from the firm before it would be official, but once again I saw the drool and knew that if I could squeak through security, the job was mine.

I signed some paperwork, including a generic waiver for a background check, and set up the second interview. We did lunch with six people and I knocked it out of the ballpark. No one was drinking, but they acted like giddy schoolgirls every time I said anything at all. At the time I didn't realize that I was being looked at to take my potential boss's position, but in retrospect I see why they were so excited. At the time I thought it was just me, and that fed my impression of how great I had come to believe I was. I had a delusion of importance that I must believe is common among twenty-somethings: I thought I had bucked the system and was smarter than any college grad who had ever come down the pike.

Before I reached my thirties, I felt that everything that happened around me was the result of my own actions. I never stopped to think that someone else's actions might have contributed. I don't think it was conceit or self-centeredness. Those are too conscious. This is more like being clueless that there are other situations out in the world besides your own. It's like seeing two people in the corner of a room full of people whispering to each other and thinking they must be talking about you. It never occurred to me that those people at lunch had some agenda other than listening to me speak—that they might have been happy to see me come on board because I would be filling the position that needed to be filled in order to send their archnemesis packing. I gradually became more aware of this phenomenon as I got more experience. These unknown influences can apply in any situation that doesn't quite make sense. When you stop to think *Why did they pick me?* or *Why didn't they pick me?* the answer might have nothing to do with you. Perhaps you were picked because no one else applied for the job (Huh? Nawww!) or maybe you weren't picked because so-and-so was sleeping with so-and-so's wife, who doesn't like you because you wore the same dress to last year's Christmas party.

The truth is you never know what is working for or against you, and all you can do is put your best foot forward and not get too big-headed about successes or take it too personally when you get shafted. That is a piece of knowledge I wish I'd had earlier in life, but if someone had tried to tell me back then, I don't suppose I would have believed them anyway.

Regardless of the reason, the company made me an offer a week later and I accepted, assuming, of course, that they had already done the background check and I was home free. I put in my two-weeks' notice with my old firm and prepared to move on.

My first day at my new job was enlightening. We had an accounting department gathering so that I could meet the twelve employees who would now be working for me. As we sat around the table, I realized that these people were afraid to speak. They were afraid of my boss—and I got an eyeful of why she had the reputation she had.

During that half-hour meeting she proceeded to humiliate three people and yell at one more. I wasn't sure at the time whether she was just showing off or if this was the norm, but I soon came to learn it was the latter. Luckily, she reserved her cruelty for the others in the department and treated me pretty well, so long as I sat and listened to her brag about herself for a couple of hours each day. I figured that was a small price to pay for immunity, and it kept me from having to work too hard. The job was easy enough with nothing new to learn, since I had already acquired the accounting skills I needed at my last position.

One week later, a nice lady came knocking on the door to my office and introduced herself as the company's human resources associate. My blood ran cold and I started to feel a case of hives coming on. My heart began to pound so loudly that I could actually hear it, but I faked a smile and pretended to be glad to meet her. She told me that the human resources department in our home office had requested a copy of my diploma. Pound . . . pound . . . pound. I continued to smile and told her, "No problem"—I would bring it in. I'm surprised that I was able to talk at all with the knot in my throat, but there it was. She smiled and left. My mind started racing.

Was it normal to request a copy of my diploma, or had they tried to check up on me and it didn't show up? Was this their way of telling me they had found me out and that I should leave before the cops show up? My panic quickly turned to paranoia as I spent the rest of the day feeling like I wanted to slink down to the sewer and toss myself in. I couldn't believe that I had left my previous job assuming all this red tape had already been handled. If I were caught now, then I would be left with no job and no leads. I'd even induced Mr. Sweaty to hang up on me!

I couldn't talk to anyone for the rest of the day. I was frozen to my desk and unable to do anything. Fear had a grip on me and was affecting my ability to think things through. I literally couldn't move. If my phone had rung, I probably wouldn't be sitting here writing now—I would have died of cardiac arrest. I was suffocating right there in my office, as if I were trapped without oxygen. I panicked and was able to come up with only one solution: I had to produce a diploma.

I had considered the legal ramifications of lying about my educational history every now and then over the years, but I had always managed to convince myself that the burden was on the company to check backgrounds, and if they didn't do so, well, then, that was their own fault. I was certain I could be terminated for lying if anyone ever found out, but probably not much else, unless you count the suffering and devastating humiliation.

Being faced with forging a document, though, opened up a whole new window of possibilities for me: What really constitutes fraud and at what point is it criminal? Do forethought and malice come into play, and, if so, do they make the sentencing tougher? I didn't know the answer to those questions and soon enough decided that I didn't *ever* want to know. I could have done some research and found the answers somewhere, but I decided I didn't need any additional pieces of information eating away at my brain like a rat at some stale cheese for the next hundred years. My desperation helped me shove the thoughts away and take action.

I had an old friend who had graduated from the college I had claimed to have attended, and she was my one and only hope. I called her up and explained my situation, and she agreed to help me out. Two days later I had a photocopy of a diploma with my name on it from a school I never graduated from, and I turned it into human resources. I never heard another word about it, but for the next two weeks I was a walking zombie.

I was paralyzed every time my phone rang and every time someone came into my office. I couldn't sleep at night and I felt as if I would never get through it.

But as the time passed with no repercussions, I learned how to control my panic and bury all fears of being caught. I trained my mind not to think about college degrees and to maintain a positive mental attitude at work. Each day I found myself thinking about my situation less, and eventually I began putting it out of my nighttime thoughts as well. Being able to control my worries is a skill that has carried me through many hard times, but it's a shame that I had to acquire it for such a negative purpose. By controlling my worries, I was also trying to bury things in my head. Unfortunately, as anyone who has ever tried to do that knows, that doesn't last long.

I got to know everyone who worked for me, especially one guy in particular. On the surface, Jack was the obvious choice for my job, but he had been overlooked. He had five years with the firm and held a bachelor's degree in accounting. He was a hard worker and very accurate and efficient. At first it was a mystery as to why he hadn't been chosen for my position. But something had motivated my boss to seek someone outside the firm. One might guess it was because he was a man, but I came to learn that that wasn't it—at least not entirely.

Jack was working a level below management, handling a huge amount of invoicing, and blowing the doors off everyone else in the same position. He had never been a manager, but that in and of itself wasn't the problem. The problem, as far as I could see, was that he couldn't handle pressure. He was one of those people who do their jobs very, very well so that everyone will leave them alone. He reminded me of myself at the craft store years earlier. He was the model employee and was happy being just that. If he was put under the gun for anything, he turned bright red and fidgeted until someone saved him from self-immolation. Ironically, he was kind of cocky and arrogant, but in a harmless sort of way.

Jack was the perfect example of an educated person who is not a leader. I think the money he forked out for college was wasted, and let's not even *start* talking about the time he spent. Everything he knew he could have learned on the job, and he had no potential to own the place. The kicker was that he would have been happy staying in his position and doing a great job forever, except other people expected him to want more!

When I was hired, everyone thought he was jealous, but I don't think that was the case. I have a feeling he was relieved—relieved that he could stay inside his comfort zone and keep doing 110 percent for the company at something he knew how to do better than anyone else.

Unfortunately, managers find it hard to believe that not everyone wants to or can learn to be a manager. They sometimes make it their personal mission to make everyone like them. I recognized this guy as very valuable at what he did and encouraged his success at that level. After I got to know him, he confided in me that he kind of liked where he was, except, of course, the glass ceiling he was hitting when it came to his salary. He was already the go-to guy for all the other people who did invoicing, so we made him *their* manager. All that consisted of was doing exactly what he was already doing.

So we added a layer to our staff without adding another person, let him keep his valuable job while still advancing in pay, hushed all of the whispering, and made it clear that I no longer needed to be directly involved in invoicing. In return, he didn't have to speak publicly or go to meetings or make decisions outside of his own comfort zone. And I had an extremely loyal, grateful, skilled employee whom everyone was happy remained on board.

I have found through the years that motivating people based on their specific needs is key to getting them to do what I need them to do. During one of our staff meetings I handed out a survey I had found in one of my management how-to books. It was a simple questionnaire that listed different motivations for what would inspire people to do their jobs. Some of the choices were money, good reviews, awards, social events, and so on. The idea was for each person to put the numbers 1 to 10 next to each item, in the order of importance to them. The results were interesting, and I used the feedback I've received over the years many times.

I saw that people have different motivations based on their lives. Not everyone was motivated by money—can you believe it? Some of them just want to know they are doing a good job. Or they want flexible hours. Or health benefits. Or an office instead of a cubicle. This enlightenment intrigued me, and I tested it out without them knowing. Sure enough, I could give smaller raises to the folks who found praise more important than money. I gave the challenging work to those who craved it, and I let the social butterflies plan our meetings and events.

It sounds so simple, but I think in corporate America people fall victim to the strict guidelines of their official job descriptions. I felt people needed outlets for the talents they possessed above and beyond what their jobs required. This kept them a little happier and served our department well.

As the months with my new firm crept on, I kept to myself, as usual. I couldn't make friends, since doing so might open the door to people wanting to know more about my history. I worked hard at bringing the accounting group together and lightening the mood in the office. My boss didn't particularly like it, since she was more concerned with finding a troll to do her dirty work. That is about when my first big promotion started to take shape.

My boss's head was on the chopping block, although neither one of us knew it when I was hired. She actually thought *she* was in line for a promotion and told me I would have her job in eighteen months. I ended up having it in six.

A group of higher-ups, most of whom had attended my second interview, had it in for her and filled me in on their intentions a month before she found out. They asked me to step in and told me the train was already out of the station and that nothing could be done to save her. I accepted the position and sat back to watch things happen. I think she knew something was going on behind her back, because she was pretty cruel even to me in those last few weeks. I had no problem hiding the info from her. That, after all, was my specialty: Look them in the eye and lie.

Any guilt I may have felt was washed away one day shortly before the holidays. My boss and I had been working with an outside vendor on a huge project. The company sent us, along with three other associates, holiday cards with several large gift certificates in them. All five cards were delivered to me, and I called her to let her know I had one for her. She flipped out and said we couldn't accept them from the vendor because the deal wasn't done and that would be bribery, blah, blah, blah. I had already looked at mine, and besides huge certificates to the new mall and restaurants built nearby, there were tickets to a football game that were, to my knowledge, unavailable anywhere else. I was bummed, but I handed them all over to her so she could return them to the vendor.

A few weeks went by and the vendor popped by my office. He asked me if I had enjoyed the football game. It didn't dawn on me what he meant, so I asked him. He said the game he had given me tickets to, of course. I told him I thought she had returned all those cards to him, and he said she had not. In fact, he had seen her—and several of her friends—at the game.

I couldn't believe someone would steal gifts from four other people like that. She must have had $5,000 worth of certificates to the mall. I never told the other three associates what she did, because I figured she was being fired anyway, so why get involved? It did, however, help me to smile—just a little—when the ax finally fell.

She ended up not being terminated, but she was removed from accounting and all forms of management and relocated into a solitary real estate position. She had, in effect, been banished from the kingdom, full of humiliation and anger, and shipped off to Siberia. She was working for the only man in the firm who still liked her, and that was that. She hated me because I had taken her place, and there was nothing I could do about that. From that point forward our paths rarely crossed until, ironically enough, near the end of my story.

My new salary was $62,000 plus bonuses, and my title was *district administrative manager*. There were three hundred people in my office, and I was third on the totem pole for many office decisions. I inherited a larger office and my own parking space. I oversaw the largest financial district in the firm, including twelve offices and sixteen employees who reported directly to me. I was thirty years old and sitting at meetings with people twice my age. My management techniques turned around my department, and the company was buzzing about it. I rebuilt bridges that had been burned in prior years and I gained a lot of attention and respect in the firm. I took on any special project that came up and got a reputation for getting things done.

We added more space in our building and renovated the seventy thousand square feet of space we already occupied. I headed up the project and in the process got to meet and impress the board of directors.

I traveled quite a bit, and people knew me in other offices across the nation. I became a regional trainer of the finance modules for our project managers, where I was able to hone my public-speaking skills and meet many important people.

For the next year I pretended to be everything I was supposed to be. My plate was so full that I didn't have time to think about anything except work. My six-year-old daughter spent a lot of time without me, either at her grandmother's or at home with her stepdad. She didn't seem to mind, and that started to bother me, as did her packing on ten pounds because of all the fast-food dinners she was eating.

At times I tried to stop the cycle, but it was useless since I always ended up having to leave town again. My only comfort was being able to buy her things, and I began spoiling her in that way constantly. She didn't know the value of a dollar, and neither—as I came to realize—did I. I ended up teaching her that buying her something meant I loved her. I was trying to make up for not being around and trying to douse the new emotion that had begun creeping into my life—guilt.

I don't know why I started feeling it, but my guess is that responsibility is part of growing up, and as time marches on we change our minds gradually about what is important to us and who we should try to be. My twenties were all about ambition and making money and climbing the ladder. They got me to where I wanted to be, but now something was changing inside me. I craved time at home with my family and even felt bad about deceiving my colleagues about my background. I no longer felt as if I was laughing all the way to the bank and I no longer thought myself clever for lying.

There were times I played out a scenario in my head about going to human resources or to my new boss and just telling the truth. But I couldn't get my mind beyond the consequences. I couldn't imagine losing what I had become and giving up my income. I couldn't imagine standing there with egg on my face and admitting what I had done. So I told myself I must have PMS or something and put those daydreams out of my head. I told myself I must perpetuate the lie for my family's sake. They enjoyed the double income we had and it would be unfair to them to take it away because I had an attack of conscience. I had made the bed and I needed to lie in it. I told myself whatever I needed to in order to help keep my nose to the grindstone in an attempt to ignore the fact that I was a phony. But the fact was, all the respect and admiration I enjoyed was built on the foundation of a lie. It wasn't real—and it could vanish at any time.

In a continuing effort to keep the guilt at bay, I became a people pleaser as well as a humanitarian. There was something about charity work that helped me redeem myself in my own eyes, especially work that encouraged higher education. I purposely chose avenues where I could work with kids and encourage them to learn about computers and to grow up to be engineers and architects.

I reviewed my employees every six months and became a broken record, telling any of them without a degree to get back to school and get one. I approved numerous requests for company reimbursment of continuing education and had two employers who told me they had gone back to school solely because I had encouraged them to do so. I felt great about that, and those were the things that got me through the days.

I had also managed to shed all the pounds I had gained earlier and was back to buying size 6 clothes. My hair was longer once again, and I could afford to have it professionally done. My shoes were always four-inch heels and my perfumes were the best money could buy. I had fake nails, a fake tan, and real diamonds on most of my fingers. These things not only helped me feel beautiful, but they also helped me look good, which was a feeling I liked a lot. The dichotomy of wanting and fearing to be real still wore on me. I wanted to be me but was afraid I didn't know who that was. Who was real—the little girl who excelled in math and science, or the femme fatale of the business world who looked like a million bucks and someday hoped she'd make it? It was a moral dilemma to which I had no response.

Still, looking good is half the battle, and that meant looking tanned. I went to the salon several times a week. I had been born an extremely pale white girl with blue eyes, yet I could actually achieve a tan in the booth. Tanning in a salon also gave me some time to rest, a power nap of sorts, when I needed it most. I felt as if I looked healthier and thinner with a tan, and I was treated well at the salon since I dropped money for all the latest and greatest products. I could breeze in, breeze out, and maintain a healthy glow. Heck, when you're phony on the inside, why not be phony on the outside too?

Clothes also gave me the same feeling. The term *power suit* had meaning to me, and the brightest spot of my day was getting dressed. I loved clothes and how they felt on my body. I loved shoes, and could have run a treadmill in heels. I loved jewelry and perfume, too, and would sometimes stand in my closet and marvel at all of the beautiful things there.

I was an addict; I lived to shop. I scoured racks looking for those special pieces that I had to have. I was selective, but never frugal. I was aware that I had recently shed weight and was beginning to receive more attention again, which only fed my desire to look the best I could. The best part was that I had already built a reputation for being smart, and then I seemed to come out of nowhere with all those good looks too. I wasn't weird skinny, not even close, but the clothes and shoes helped disguise any misplaced bulges and gave me the confidence to walk with a spring in my step.

Not all of the women in the office took my looks in stride, but I hardly cared. In fact, that was just added proof that I could finally believe what I saw in the mirror. I enjoyed the power my looks gave me, and I hate to admit that I used it whenever I needed an added "bump." It was almost like wearing a costume. I felt as if no one could see who I really was under all those clothes, and it was fun. It became my armor in the days to come and served me well.

# CHAPTER NINE

At times I stopped and wondered how I got there. How had I let everything get this far? But, more importantly, how had everyone around me let it get this far? How could I sail through the daily grind of a high-powered executive when the whole kit and caboodle was based on a lie? Sure, fake it 'til I make it. A great battle cry, but when called on the carpet, exactly how was I pulling it off? Why wasn't anyone questioning my ability, and, most of all, how was I able to do a job that required a college education when I didn't have one?

And then it dawned on me: leadership. I had an innate ability to lasso others into helping me toward my goals. Leadership is not some contrived concept achieved only by people with the ability to predict the future and create a conscious plan to get there. It's a gift that comes naturally and supersedes any real-world obstacles. It is an inborn ability to build a team dedicated to whatever common goal they are striving toward.

There is no question that there are good leaders and bad leaders, the difference being only in their goals. That discounts any rationale that the morality of the goal has anything to do with the capacity of the leader. Leaders can appear on either team, no matter what the game. Leaders do not stop and think *What would a leader do?* They simply do. If their followers were to see even a moment of uncertainty in their leaders' eyes, all would likely be lost. People want to follow those who know what they are doing. If they have to stop and think, the crucial moment of true leadership is lost.

Leaders make decisions in a nearly subliminal way. To them, there is only one direction and therefore no forks in the road. They go after goals without overthinking the consequences of their actions. They take uncalculated risks that no one will ever believe they didn't think through beforehand. They forge ahead knowing that people are behind them, without having to look back to see for sure. They possess certain personality traits that serve them well and lure others into their journey.

I exhibited some of these traits, mostly by accident, over the next several years, and I believe that is why I was able to perpetuate my lie for so long. Sometimes the traits appeared because of a natural flow of events, but other times they appeared because I was actually trying to cover up my inadequacies. This puzzles me greatly, because I will never know what kind of manager or leader I would have been had I actually graduated from college.

Luck is something all leaders rely on, even if they don't know it. My mother used to tell me I could fall into a pile of crap and come out smelling like a rose. Sure, I had some runs of bad luck once in a while, but otherwise I lived a charmed life. If I really wanted something, I would eventually get it. I didn't understand failure and I didn't understand giving up. If I was failing it didn't feel real and I could never accept it. The glass was always half full, and I counted on lady luck to get me through when I didn't have any other plan. Someone telling me no usually meant my ultimate goal would be delayed, but it was never forsaken. With luck in your pocket, nothing is a brick wall; there are merely bumps in the road.

Humility is a trait of a true leader that is often discounted these days. Working hard at something inspires others to work hard and makes them see that you believe in what you are doing. Ironically, I worked harder than I would have had I been a college grad because I was trying to compensate for what I perceived to be my inadequacies. The people I worked with, and especially those who worked for me, saw someone willing to get in there and get her hands dirty. They respected that and admired my lack of egomania. It brought them closer to me, even though it was designed to keep them at arm's length. I was unwittingly exhibiting leadership qualities while trying to cover up what I perceived as my overall lack of ability.

I never discounted anyone's job, no matter the level. I took their situations seriously and helped them work through anything that was frustrating them. I kept tabs on everyone and their satisfaction with their work. I used my skill at reading people to determine what motivated each one of them and threw them bones when I needed to. My administrative team thrived under my management skills, and I never lost an employee unless I had to terminate him or her.

Each quarter the firm had a company-wide meeting during which prizes were given out for whatever funny little contests the higher-ups decided to run. The prize this year was lunch with one of the company's top managers. I was added to the list of managers and was blown away by the concept. I attended the meeting and sat back and watched as three hundred employees competitively played a trivia game, vying to win lunch with . . . *me*. It seemed so strange, so odd that these people would vie for an hour of my time. They cheered and laughed, and everyone had a good time. The table that finally won was ecstatic, and we ended up having a great lunch the following week.

I felt honored to have been chosen and tried to live up to their expectations. They wanted to know what I thought about this and that and what I knew about the other. Some were older than I, but didn't seem fazed by it. They complimented my management style and told me the office was always buzzing about what great work my team did. I was proud of myself that day. I wonder what those people would have thought had I spilled my guts right there. Maybe I would have been their hero. I doubt it. They probably would have wished they had won lunch with someone else. Nevertheless, it was a little bit of hero worship, and I relished in it for the moment.

I know I was a good leader, too, because I had a habit of hiring people who were smarter than I. I actively sought out people who were overqualified for the position they were applying for and told them during their interviews that they should reach for my job. The upside to hiring these people seemed obvious—I always had folks around who could step in and do anything I didn't know how to do. And if they were great at it, I still got kudos for hiring them. It was a win-win situation and helped me form a tremendous bond with my team.

I had no problem hiring people who most managers would have perceived as threats to their own livelihood. I needed these people on my team to make sure I was doing the right thing.

Hiring these people helped free up my time and kept me available for any promotions that might pop up. My team was strong enough to go it alone and able to handle the workload, so I could do other things that helped keep me on the radar of the higher-ups.

I had an assistant who was the polar opposite of me—at least, of the phony me. She was very emotional, sensitive, and talkative. She knew everyone else's business. She wanted to save the world and was offended by some of the silliest situations. She was a great balance for me, and I appreciated her insight on many topics. If I had a meeting to attend where I had to lay down the law, I ran it by her first, and she pointed out some areas of my speech or plan that might "upset" people further down the ladder for reasons I hadn't even thought of. As a result, I unfurled my plans spiced with her suggestions, which made me appear more sensitive, and I was able to please more people.

Her perspectives were always enlightening, and I was often fascinated by the depth of her character. I believe if she and I sat down and did those flash cards where we had to name the first thing that came to mind, our answers would never be the same. That was a great asset during my tenure, and I knew it. Besides, I knew she was for real, and since I was a phony, I was appreciative of that. She worshiped me in a good way and I made her job as pleasant as I could.

My staff served the rest of the firm and I wanted them to be friendly, attentive, accurate, and efficient. I rewarded any actions toward these goals and acted quickly if someone fell outside the boundaries of my plan. I treated my employees with respect and paid them as well as I could. The company had guidelines for every position, of course, and those for whom I felt the maximum salary fell short I would compensate in other ways. I had picnics and outings and happy hours and anything else I could think of to help keep the team cohesive and productive. We spent a little extra on better coffee and I didn't watch the clock if they were a little late. I was invited to their weddings and privy to their private lives. I was someone they could go to and dump on if they were having a bad day. These people were important to me because they handled the everyday details that made me look good.

I was also able to recognize the importance of each person's function within the group. I knew that some of my employees were sometimes useless when it came to doing their jobs as defined in the company's official job description, but I also knew they could prove vital when it came to making people laugh when the going got tough. Those people who can't seem to stop making the same typo over and over again can be worth their weight in gold if they can lighten up the mood at the worst of times.

And let's not discount the mother hen. She might not be the fastest worker, or computer literate, but let's face it: She makes everyone feel like someone at work cares about them.

These people were all crucial pieces of the team, and firing them based on their job performance—as outlined by their official job description—would have been a fatal mistake. Keeping them around showed depth and compassion and kept everybody moving forward peacefully. I think some leaders get so caught up in quantifying their employees based on achievement marked on a scorecard that they forget they need followers to be a leader. Everyone needs a role, and it is the leader's job to keep everyone busy. That realization introduced me to my favorite pastime: delegating.

Delegating was something I took to quickly and easily. I found that I had hired the correct people—people more educated than I was—and they were actually happy to take on the more challenging work as long as it wasn't grunt work. They were actually flattered if I asked them to do something that should have fallen on me. *Flattered.* They took pride in each assignment, hoping it would get them kudos for doing well. I never let them down. My faith in their abilities allowed me to volunteer myself at management meetings for any project that needed to be done.

I began to see that it wasn't important whether or not I'd had experience doing a particular job, so long as someone on my team had. We could analyze, we could proof, and we could throw a charity golf tournament that rivaled any outing anywhere. I was able to assign my group to anything that came down the pike, because every time I hired someone I was looking for my replacement. My employees felt challenged in their roles, not pigeonholed. I wish I could say I did this all for the greater good, but honestly, I did it because I had to. Either way, I got credit for it, as did my team.

I also soon learned that I have a natural talent for problem solving. I am an out-of-the-box thinker, all about finding the solution. I have the tenacity of a bulldog, working until a problem is solved, and extreme patience when it comes to debating the appropriate solutions. Sometimes my ideas would be used, sometimes not. But most times, they would at least spark some new thinking on whatever the issue was and get things going in the right direction.

Staying positive was a trait that I had learned toward the end of my custody battle. Appearing strong and confident in the face of adversity was difficult and grew even more so as my responsibilities expanded. I approached everything as if I genuinely cared about it and I did everything with heart and compassion whenever possible. If I knew someone was upset, I would swing by his office to discuss something positive with him. If I had a bad day at home—which also was becoming more and more frequent—I didn't let it affect my day at work. I know most people work to do the opposite of that, but I was not most people. I was predictably upbeat and invited into many arenas for that reason. I had people from different departments come to me with ideas and ask me to come to meetings just so I could sit and nod my approval. They felt this increased the chance that everyone would buy into it. That's pretty powerful stuff, and I enjoyed my growing reputation.

One part about leadership that I did *not* enjoy was doing the tough duties when they arose. Firing people was never a bright spot, even if the person deserved it. However, I eventually learned to do it without emotion and without thinking about it too much afterward. I found it helped keep their crying to a minimum if I acted calmly and reasonably.

I fired six people over the years, only one of whom brought it on herself. She was a relatively new high-ranking employee with tenure of six months. She was degreed and in fact had previously taught accounting at a school before entering corporate America. She was friendly, albeit a little odd now and then, but likable, and she fit into the team fairly well. She handled a good amount of invoicing for my department and she did okay with it most of the time.

Then one day a package was returned by UPS with a bad address on it. There was no name on the sending address, just the firm's name, so the package went to me to find out what it was and who it needed to get to. I opened the package and found a pen inside. The letter with the pen indicated that it had been won in an eBay auction and was being mailed to the recipient. The letter was from the employee in my department. The problem was that she had charged the shipment to our firm's business account. This was not out of the ordinary, so long as we indicated "personal" on the shipping label so that the bill could be charged back to the individual, but this gal had instead indicated it should be billed to a particular project number. At first glance it appeared as if she was trying to have the firm pay for her shipment. I decided to look into it further before confronting her about it.

I checked the project detail for the projects she handled billing for, and, sure enough, there was an unusually large number of UPS charges on most of them over the prior several months. I pulled the records of the shipping labels and discovered that the addresses were random individuals who had nothing to do with the projects being billed. It definitely appeared that this woman was running her own little eBay business and charging the shipping fees to the firm, with no intention of paying us back.

I was furious. My initial reaction was to walk down the hall and fire her, but I held back for a few moments. I couldn't believe that someone would risk her entire livelihood for a few measly shipping fees. She made enough money to pay for them herself, and that meant she was just doing it because she could. She was doing it with intent to steal. She thought she had found a loophole and made a conscious decision to take advantage of it.

I called human resources and told them about the situation. They asked what I wanted to do, and I quickly made the decision to terminate her. I did it that afternoon. I confronted her with the documentation I had discovered and asked her if she had any explanation for it.

She said she did not. I told her she was terminated, effective immediately, and she calmly got up and left. She didn't apologize or look surprised. She looked angry. Maybe she was angry at herself, but my mind's eye was telling me that she was angry at me for finding her out. It bothered me that she didn't have the ability to look at herself and say, "Hey what I did was wrong."

The problem was, here I was living a much bigger lie than someone misappropriating a few small shipping charges, and I terminated someone based on a zero-tolerance policy for such poor judgment. Where was the line for what I was supposed to forgive? Should I have given her a second chance because I was a phony and should have been able to sympathize? I didn't think so. Perhaps, though, I had terminated her so decisively because I wanted to keep up my image—to help hide my own deception. I wasn't sure that was the case, but how would I ever know? Had my imaginary image created some imaginary moral code that I would uphold even if it made me a hypocrite? Was I nothing more than a drunk driver hiding behind a MADD bumper sticker in hopes it would make me less likely to get pulled over?

Later that evening I sat and thought about the situation. I rationalized my self-doubt by concluding that she was stealing—taking something that did not belong to her. Stealing is far different than what I was doing. Stealing was wrong and had to be dealt with. I thought back to Sunday school and the Ten Commandments. *Thou shalt not steal* was a serious commandment, but *Thou shalt not lie?* Come on—since when? Stealing was right up there with *Thou shalt not kill*. I mean, even God must have understood that people were going to have to lie from time to time. Stealing, I convinced myself, was different.

The next day at work I got kudos for handling the situation as quickly and forcefully as I had. We docked the shipping fees out of her last paycheck, and we never heard about the matter again.

Someone once told me that she thought it was endearing that I didn't have my degree hanging in my office, since she always thought that was intimidating to others. I told her I didn't want my employees to feel as if I thought I was better than they simply because I had a degree. Another lie, but heck, at that point, what did it matter? It was just another instance where I appeared to be a good leader, but increasingly I was beginning to see that I was just a good liar.

But, liar or not, I knew that I had to keep my true identity secret. Toward that goal, I was a driven woman. I made friends with human resources managers in high places and kept up on all the latest policy changes that could affect me.

On the surface, my ties to those people made me look as though I cared about their thankless jobs. I appeared compassionate to their cause of keeping emotions in the workforce—stopping us nonemotional types from acting without considering the feelings of others. In reality, I was using my relationships with them just exactly as I was using my relationships with everyone else in the company—to hide the fact that I was a phony.

It amazes me to this day to realize that I was developing into a top-flight manager, not so much because of the leadership qualities I possessed, but because of my need to cover up my lack of education. Of course, leadership happens whether it is contrived or not. People pay attention to everything a leader does and interpret it all as they believe it fits into their lives. I don't know if a leader can be created, and I don't know if leadership can be faked. It may sound as if I was faking it, but I'm guessing that would be impossible.

If we could create a list of all of the things leaders do consistently, I don't think someone who is not a natural leader could do them all and get the same results. The moments of indecision that arise when the stakes are high would weed out those who couldn't handle it. The ability to read people and to sacrifice some along the way for the benefit of others would be too challenging for the average phony. The bottom line was that I was good at being a manager. By delegating and hiring the right people, I could concentrate my efforts on doing that one thing and doing it well. I didn't get so tangled up in the details that I couldn't make decisions, and I was able to keep my eye on the ball because I had people watching everything else for me. I was never too busy to take on new things, and this made me valuable to my company. I had true value; I was an asset.

Of course, I also relied on the fact that I was able to fly under the radar for so long because most of our employees were so absorbed in their own messed-up lives that they hardly had time to think about anyone or anything else. If they did find time, I was the last person they would take that time to look into. I appeared to function well on my own, never complained, and never failed to reach my goals.

In the big picture, I am a combination of a true leader and a contrived one. I think the only credit I can give to my phony persona is that it made me try harder. I threw myself into my work because I had to. The kicker was that I also excelled at it.

# CHAPTER TEN

The number of extramarital affairs that occur in corporate America is mind-boggling. Whether it was barely flirting or out-and-out cheating, most executives' personal lives put them in the same position I found myself in—having to cover their butts when the going got dicey. The rumor mill, as it was lovingly called, kept everyone abreast of who was doing what with whom, and that was enough to keep most employees on their toes.

But not everyone, of course. Even I fell victim to a brief extramarital affair at one point, so who was I to pass blame? It was an extremely painful experience and something very easy to get wrapped up in and sidetracked by. I got caught up in a whirlwind romance with another manager. I wasn't looking for anything permanent or even real. In fact, being a phony helped me to shove any thoughts of reality or possible consequences under the table. I simply had to live for the moment, to enjoy the *now* of an exciting new relationship without ever having to stop to think about the *later*. When everything seems fleeting and temporary, an affair seems natural.

I figured that having an affair was just one more thing that businesspeople do, so it was okay for me to do. I went so far in rationalizing the relationship that I actually began to believe it was preordained. It was something I was supposed to do. I told myself I had exhibited plenty of self-control, but things had just gotten out of hand. I viewed it as an out-of-body experience. It was someone I had an instant reaction to. I swear I heard a "boom" the first time we laid eyes on each other, and he swore the same.

He was extremely handsome and charming and a great kisser. When I was in his arms I could forget the world, and I did so often. He became my escape from reality. And the sex . . . I saw a special on animal planet not too long ago about badgers. Apparently badgers have the best sex of any animals in the world. They go at it like . . . well, badgers. With him, I was no longer the Ice Princess, and I no longer acted like one.

Hiding the affair was simple: I used my finely honed acting skills, and all the while the affair helped to distract me from paying attention to my newly discovered conscience. I could continue my charade and live up to my reputation even behind closed doors. What could be more perfect?

The person with whom I began carrying on didn't know I was a phony, of course, so I never had to worry about confronting that issue with him. I didn't have to worry about protecting him or buying things for him. I could simply be the sexy big-shot corporate spitfire others had begun to see me as. Guys dug it, and he was no exception. I quickly wrapped myself in the image, and it was fun knowing how desirable I was to him. Badger wanted me because of who he thought I was and how forbidden we were together. All fake. All phony. Right up my alley.

He wasn't the first man to hit on me, of course. Numerous others had let their intentions be known, one way or another, over the years. Some were sly and charming, others were painfully awkward. I found that men expected me to notice if they stared too long or touched my hand. I was usually too wrapped up in what I was trying to accomplish, though, at least most of the time.

I taught several courses of up to thirty engineers at a time, training them to use our company's accounting software. Each course took a couple of days, so I'd have to spend an evening in a hotel in the town where I happened to be teaching. I remember one class in particular in which a guy from my home office attended. I was talking to him afterward and asked him how he thought I did. He said I did great and that all the guys had been raving about me. I flushed with pride and felt extremely gratified. Then he clarified his statement by telling me how hot all the guys had thought I was.

Hot? Me? I was stunned. I realized suddenly that they probably hadn't heard a word I'd said but enjoyed the class because I was a good-looking woman. I laughed off the comment, but I was really hurt deep inside.

I went to numerous company functions and danced with far too many men whose excitement I could feel on my leg. I am not sure what kind of message they hoped to get across with their show of interest, but it was one of the more common messages I received.

Of all the conversations I had alone with men, nearly half resulted in some sort of pass—an offer for dinner or lunch, or some other desperate plea for me to meet them for a drink to talk about their problems. I always declined . . . well, nearly always. I don't know why I gave in to this one person, but I did. He seemed as alone as I was and was relatively safe since he was married too. Or so I thought.

What I didn't think was how much pain my infidelity would cause. It was as if I decided to play around with fire in the hope of getting burned. My loneliness made me an easy player. I needed affection so badly. I needed to feel wanted so badly that I didn't care what form it took. I wanted to hear all the superficial lines and feel pretty. I wanted to feel anything besides the guilt and loneliness that plagued me daily.

As the months passed, the superficial part of our affair started to take a backseat to true affection for each other. I am certain I was his outlet as much as he was mine, but it was becoming more than that.

We were spending more time together, and chunks of that time were spent talking and getting to know one another. The "boom" happened every time he walked in the room, and I had grown addicted to it. I couldn't trust my heart, though—I didn't know how. He was a similar creature and therefore also not one to trust his emotions.

There we were, trying to keep it fun, but sinking deeper and deeper into love. I decided to tell him my secret. I think it was a test I thought no one could pass. It was my way of destroying something I couldn't seem to let go of—before it destroyed me. He was holding me in his arms one night and I confessed to him that I had never gone to college. I couldn't see his face, since I was nuzzled up under his neck, but I didn't feel his embrace falter at all. He didn't flinch.

Nothing changed between us; if anything, our bond was stronger. He had become a friend I had never had before. I had handed him the ability to destroy me, and I wasn't even worried about it. He was in this secret with me and saw me for what I was. We had passion, romance, and trust in one another. Unfortunately, we also had spouses.

The affair ended in disaster, of course. My husband found out and my life became a living hell for the next several months. Both Badger and I decided to stay with our respective families, in an attempt to do the right thing. It is too painful for me to rehash in detail, but my husband decided to forgive me and we moved on with our marriage. I spent much of the next few years trying to forget Badger and what it had felt like to be loved for who I really was.

Badger never told anyone my secret, even when things ended so horribly. I am both grateful for and surprised by that. Loyal people always have a way of impressing me.

The bottom line is that I came to realize nearly everyone had some sort of issue they didn't want others to know about, and that made them less different than me than I originally thought. In fact, I am certain that I would have found many people's skeletons even more devastating than mine, had they ever come to light.

Of course, we were a large company, so scandal was bound to strike from time to time. Every now and again, someone's naked pictures would circulate on the Internet or someone else would get arrested for beating his kids or driving drunk. We live in an imperfect world, and perfect people are not part of it. Most of the things these people did were merely a form of stress relief. Ironically enough, I'll bet much of the stress probably arose from their jobs, which ended up being among the first things to be destroyed.

# CHAPTER ELEVEN

ON and OFF. That was how I operated. I consciously had these two modes. My ON mode kicked in when I was working. I was upbeat, witty, charming, and unflappable. Operating in this mode was exhausting. I could be ON for only so many hours in a row before I started to physically wear out. I would then find some time and space to turn OFF for a while. My OFF mode meant being alone and recharging my batteries: wearing sweats and reading a gory horror novel.

Looking back, I see this as a step in my conscious mind toward letting the real me start to come out. Mind you, I never let it come out when anyone else was around, but at least I was no longer trying to fool myself 100 percent of the time. I was becoming more and more aware that my ON mode was an act. I was simply playing a part that I had created back during a time when I didn't know how difficult it would be to maintain that role forever.

There were times when I found myself walking toward a meeting and, right before entering, I would think to myself, *Ok, you're ON—smile!* I would then walk in beaming. I was very aware of how much effort it had begun to take to feign interest in certain subjects. I knew just how to make appropriate eye contact and what facial expressions to rely upon in order to appear excited or intrigued. It reminded me of the games I played as a kid, when I consciously tried to change someone's perception of me. Sometimes I concentrated so much on how my face looked that I wasn't even listening to what was being said.

I began craving OFF time more and more and dreaded certain situations where I had to be ON for too long. I no longer bothered to be

ON at home, and it was refreshing. My daughter didn't seem to notice or mind the difference, and that was encouraging. My husband played video games most of the time in the evening, so he didn't notice either.

I wonder how many people have OFF and ON modes and no one else knows it? Or is it a different layer of awareness brought on only by the need to hide one's true self? Can a person have two totally different personalities depending on what situation she is in? And what happens if those two worlds collide somehow? Was I really a bubbly, chipper, get-the-job-done type-A personality? Is that something that can even be faked? And if it can, why doesn't everyone fake it? My guess is that they can't act or they don't want to—or they have managed their lives to the point of being themselves, for better or worse. Are there actually people who can do that?

At any given meeting, how many people can walk into a room as they really are and how many walk in masquerading as someone they're not? It's impossible to tell.

How many people have an ON and OFF switch and how many people use it to cover up something we would all be shocked to know? I'm guessing there are more than a few. Are we overachievers simply because of our constant need to overcompensate for some real or perceived shortcoming? Should we stop and take a look at who is trying too hard and question their motives? Or are there people in the workforce who truly work harder because that is who they really are all the time?

Being ON made me more money. Being OFF did nothing for me except to awaken in me the realization that I hate being ON.

But my true feelings had little bearing on my life. I had to continue to turn ON and OFF if I wanted to continue my success. ON had all the upside but wore me out. I needed some extended OFF time—and I needed it soon.

# CHAPTER TWELVE

Vacation. It seemed like a splendid idea. Maybe all the doubt I was beginning to feel about my life and my career was merely a reaction to the stress brought on by working too hard. Not that I had never taken a few days off of work, but I had never gone anywhere to *get away*. Suddenly the notion of traveling somewhere far away from the business world seemed the perfect opportunity to steal a little extra time with my family and be OFF for a while.

I did manage to take some business trips that I tried to turn into minivacations. My husband especially loved trips to Las Vegas. Luckily I had business there and could fund part of our trip as a business expense.

When we traveled, we rarely took more than a long weekend, but I was okay with that because I found myself unable to relax and enjoy the time away from home anyway. If I tried to gamble, I felt as if I couldn't win because I was making money in a dishonest way. If I tried relaxing on a beach somewhere, my thoughts would start racing about what might be happening back at the office. Could someone have found me out since I wasn't there to control the situation? Were new background-check decisions being made that I wasn't there to veto?

I had to stay checked into work and felt I had to be present and working for things to remain secret. Vacation was too much time to myself, too much time for self-discovery—and that meant only self-doubt for someone in my position. I had a BlackBerry and was an addict back before it was common. I wanted to be involved in everything and joined committees and volunteered for task forces just so I could keep tabs on everything that might be happening that could affect me.

Looking back, I wish I could have taken more vacations with my family, and I wish I could have enjoyed the ones I did take. I never stopped working or thinking about work, even when I wasn't there. I just couldn't let go. I've heard the phrase "having a lot of balls in the air," and I liken that to what I felt. I felt like my lie was a ball in the air, and if I wasn't there to keep it afloat, it could drop. The thought was constantly on my mind, and it destroyed any chance I had to relax, including on vacation. I had to read my e-mails and check my voice-mails and call the office regularly just to make sure no one sounded "odd" to me or had stopped taking my calls. My family must have thought I was crazy.

Not being able to relax on vacation was clearly a symptom of my phoniness anxiety. I couldn't stand to be alone with myself with nothing to do, because then I had time to think things to death. How ironic is it that the one fruit of labor I should be sitting back and enjoying—the vacation—is the one I couldn't indulge myself in! Vacations are an integral part of a businessperson's life, giving overworked employees a chance to unwind and get some stress out of their lives.

My vacations did just the opposite for me. I returned to work a paranoid mess, more frazzled than when I left. My inability to unwind would catch up with me eventually.

In time, we simply stopped taking family vacations. I made up excuses to avoid them, and my family always "understood."

In retrospect, I believe I had so much trouble unwinding because I was aware that I was doing something *wrong*. Of course that's true, but coming to the realization had serious implications for me.

We learn as very small children the difference between right and wrong. Wrong is wrong no matter what, and whether or not we believe in God, we still know right from wrong. It is a fundamental value that cannot be argued with. The number of people who literally can't differentiate between right and wrong is so small that it is virtually nonexistent. Someone who truly cannot tell right from wrong is considered so aberrant that he isn't even liable for his actions to the same extent as a sane person in a court of law.

I knew that what I was doing was wrong from the start, and I was clearly making a choice to keep deceiving everyone I knew.

The fact that there was no obvious victim to my wrongdoing began to become more of an excuse than a comfort. It was wrong to lie and I knew it. It was wrong to accept my paycheck based on who my employer thought I was. It was wrong to masquerade as someone who had been trained to do what I was doing. It was wrong to lie to my daughter. It was wrong to lie to my husband. Knowing it was wrong made it impossible for me to take any pride in what I had accomplished. Taking a vacation made it impossible for me to avoid coming face-to-face with my guilt.

I realize now that I used to seek out people who were proud of me because I couldn't be proud of myself. Those early days when I felt a certain amount of pride in beating the system were over. The short road no longer held any excitement for me. Doing the wrong thing was simply wrong, even if there were no true "victims."

I felt I was at a moral crossroads in my life. I could no longer ignore the fact that I had another persona somewhere inside of me, and that person was a good person. I wanted to do what was *right*. I just didn't know how. I needed a little shove in the right direction. As with many things in life, I should have watched what I wished for, because I was about to get it.

# CHAPTER THIRTEEN

In July 2004, things started happening quickly. Trouble was brewing in another district, and the person there who held the same title as I was fired. I was asked to cover the district until the company could find a replacement. It was a big job, but of course I said I would do it.

My new responsibility meant even more time away from home, and after four months of babysitting the position, I was offered a promotion that would make me responsible for both districts permanently. The CFO told me I could write my own ticket, so I asked for an apartment in that district, since I would be there so much. I also asked for a personal automobile paid in full ($18,000), five hundred shares of company stock, a new title, and an even larger salary. It was done.

I suddenly found myself overseeing the two largest financial districts in the firm and had a lot more on my plate than I had ever expected.

My boss sent out an e-mail to all thirty-five hundred employees announcing my promotion. The best part of the announcement was the opening line. It called me a "natural leader." For the first time in my life, I realized that I really *was* a leader and that, educated or not, I was a valuable person and a prized employee at my firm. Up until I read those words, I thought every good thing about me wasn't really true because everything was based on a lie. Those words touched me as none had ever before.

But the good times and basking in Florida's proverbial sunshine were short-lived. Within weeks, a series of devastating hurricanes pummeled the Panhandle State. They kept coming, and the damage was widespread. My firm led a large operation for cleanup and damage control. We hired four hundred temporary employees, and, when all was said and done, billed out more than $40 million in fees. All of the financial pieces to the puzzle fell to me, and I stepped up to handle them the best I could.

The pace was fast and frenzied, and it tested all of my abilities and patience. Everyone was under the gun, and the need for strong, decisive leadership was never greater. I slept very little and was home even less.

With the help of some other key people from the firm, we waded our way through the disaster and still managed to keep up with our work. Our efforts did not go unnoticed. Our board of directors cited me for my part in the disaster projects. It was quite a feather in my managerial cap. It was also a bit scary. Each month I was responsible for an enormous amount of money, coming and going. Each day I scanned numerous hundred-page reports trying to uncover mistakes that could have cost the company time and money.

Toward the end of the projects, I made a mistake. A *big* one. I took someone's word that we had a signed contract in-house for some work we had done up front. I should have checked the paperwork myself, but I was in too big of a hurry.

I had recognized $400,000 in revenue for the company and found out a few days later, after the deadline for closing our books, that there was no contract to cover it. It is a big no-no to recognize revenue without a signed contract. I panicked and called the CFO, my boss, and told him what had happened. I must have been hyperventilating, because he told me to relax and to breathe deeply. Everything would be okay.

Of course, it wasn't *his* butt on the line, so I didn't sleep for the next three weeks while contract negotiations were worked through, but it finally ended up okay.

After that, I began to question my competence. I began to wonder whether I was in over my head. Did I really have the right stuff to be handling what I was handling? And if I screwed up, was it a direct result of not being smart enough? Of not being educated enough? Or were these things that happened to everyone?

I suddenly found myself longing for those days of yore when I felt invincible. I was flooded with self-doubt. And I felt something for the first time in my entire corporate career: lack of the drive to do better.

It had been so much easier before, so much more fun. The more I did, the more money I made. The more money I made, the more I enjoyed life and savored my role in the limelight.

Now something else was occupying my thoughts. Just how much responsibility was I capable of handling? How much work could I do until something went horribly wrong? How much more could I take?

I spent my evenings trying to sleep, but it rarely happened. I felt my physical and emotional health beginning to fail. Could I pull through it all? Was this my just reward for having lied my way through the system? Was I about to collapse?

Yet, despite my innermost fears, I managed to continue on with my workload. Somehow I made it through each day without another major catastrophe. And I must have looked pretty good doing it, at least on the outside, because the corporate bigwigs took notice, and my rise up the corporate ladder was about to take another quantum leap.

I learned one day in the middle of all the hurricane relief work that I had been elected into the Leadership Class for that year. Nominations had to come from a previous Leadership Class member—I heard I received two of them—and final acceptance is voted on by the board of directors.

Now, I have never been big on pomp and circumstance, but the Leadership Class is a very high honor. Only twenty-five people out of thirty-five hundred are chosen each year—fewer than 1 percent. It's a program designed to coach the next generation of leaders in the company—the next generation of corporate stars. As one of the participants, I was flown to meetings all around the country, attending talks on different subjects such as mergers/acquisitions, project management, and ethics.

Yes, *ethics*.

During the year the firm also supplies each recipient with a personal life and career coach and expects everyone to take part in a class project. The coaches are not employees of the firm but are usually retired businesspeople who have achieved a high degree of success in various walks of life. Their goal, of course, is to help train the next generation of corporate leaders (and maybe, just a little, to collect their fees of $200 an hour for chatting with us on the telephone).

At first, I was leery. After all, I had made a career out of not letting people into my head, but the firm made it clear that anything that is said remains confidential.

My coach sent me some typical psychiatric and personality tests so that we could get to know each other, at least on paper. He asked about my family and my life balance. He gave me a tool that I will never again be without in my life: a pie chart illustrating what is important to me and the concept of balancing it based on happiness. It came to be known as my Happy Pie.

We determined that the three things that made my life tick were family, money, and career. We made three pieces of pie, each representing one of these areas of my life. The coach then explained that these three pieces of pie should ideally be equal in importance, and only when they were would I be truly happy. He said I needed to determine what size each piece of my life was currently, and then I would know what areas needed improvement.

It sounds far too simple to work, but I use this pie method to this day and it has never let me down. It's a very effective way of seeing at a glance just where your life is today as opposed to where you'd like it to be.

I sat in my office for hours trying to determine what sizes my pie slices were. It was an exercise that forced me to be honest with myself—for one of the few times in my life—about how I really felt about each of the pieces. Finally, I could gather my thoughts about three unrelated issues and put them in a simple chart. It was something I could get my mind around, something so simple in design that would point me in the right direction. I could be honest making my pie because I didn't have to share it with anyone except my coach.

Not surprisingly, my pie at the time was anything but balanced. My money piece was the largest, my career piece about half that size, and my family piece was a mere sliver. Seeing that nearly broke my heart, but it gave me the knowledge I needed to begin making a change. It gave me something to focus on doing right. It also validated my unhappiness with my life as a whole. It was out of balance, and my Happy Pie proved it. I wasn't being silly or selfish or lazy—I merely had an out-of-whack Happy Pie!

I spoke with the coach about my daughter's weight gain and how I hated traveling so much, and he encouraged me to take a look at my life and question whether or not I was where I wanted to be. He said things out loud that I had only dared to think in my head. He stressed the importance of my family and how poisonous the business world can be to personal relationships. I never told him about my lie, but he became the voice in my head that started allowing me to tell people no when they asked too much of me at work.

My coach soon became the mentor I needed most, because he had my best interests at heart—not merely the interests of the corporate front office. He asked me tough questions and wouldn't let me hide behind all my stock reasons for being away from my family. He pointed out that, although spoiled financially, my family would choose me if they had to choose between the person or the cash. Did I already know this? Perhaps—and perhaps not. I knew what my coach was talking about, and I knew he was right. I set out to fix my Happy Pie.

My first Leadership Class session was on the subject of—what else?—ethics. It was a two-day course with several lectures on what ethics meant to our organization.

We heard from my boss as well as other corporate board members. We discussed everything from embezzlement and harassment to downloading free music from the Internet. We played a grown-up version of Truth or Dare. We were asked questions with the understanding that no one outside would ever find out what our answers were. Apparently, truly ethical people do the right thing even when no one is looking! That is what was expected of us as the next generation of leaders.

The tone in the room was one of zero tolerance for unethical activities. They told us stories of executives at other firms who had been caught doing unethical things and how quickly they fell once discovered. Our chairman of the board spoke at length about how he himself knew where every single dime had gone in the firm for the past twenty years. He seemed very confident that his group of leaders was trustworthy and ethical. He also made it sound as if he checked up on everyone's activities behind the scenes.

I was impressed by the speeches and longed to be sitting up front with the other corporate brass. I wanted to feel like one of them. In reality, I shouldn't have been in the same room. I felt throughout it all that everyone else was better than I. They had all earned their places there and deserved them, while I had made it in on a lark. They could speak about morals and ethics and really believe in what they were saying, while I could only fake it. They had carried the firm through the years without falling victim to temptations that could have harmed themselves and the firm. I am certain that all of them had access to situations in which they could have made the wrong choice and didn't, simply because they were ethical. At that time I did not realize that there was someone else in that room who had failed that challenge miserably.

We discussed leadership and what being a leader really means. We talked about how some of the best leaders in the world were not those with master's degrees or doctorates but rather people with the personality and ability to rally others together to make the machine run more smoothly. I sat there in my chair wanting to scream. There I was, working for a firm that was obviously progressive enough to realize that education is not what makes a good leader, and yet I was already tied into my fabrication with no way out except to expose my unethical ways and lose my job, never mind my ability to be a leader for my company. I was angry at myself—and somehow angry at them too. Life has a way of really sticking it to you.

After sitting through the meeting, I had a new perspective on leadership. I had already come to grips with the fact that I was a natural leader but was very frustrated that companies had to have meetings to point out that undereducated people could be leaders too. It was brilliantly simple and certainly had all the *oomph* to be the next latest and greatest concept in management. In a sense, I was living proof that education had nothing to do with being a great leader. This meant that there was something else involved; there was some kind of magic combination of qualities that separated the leaders from the followers, and education was not on the list. Or was it?

All these thoughts did nothing but make me feel a day late and a dollar short. More than ever, I wanted to tell on myself and see what would happen. There were times when I came close to picking up the phone, but I could never bring myself to dial the numbers.

I continued in my leadership role and the daunting task of doing the work of two people. My take-home pay was more than enough, and my husband was making nearly the same. It seemed strange to me that he had made it the honest way with only an associate's degree. That made me pretty proud of him—and a little envious.

We weren't letting our good fortune go unrewarded at home. We ate like kings. We had lobster on a whim and bought pretty much anything we wanted. I spent half my days in town and the other half away. I was the darling of my firm, and I spoke to my boss once or twice every few months just to hear what a great job I was doing. I had no enemies, unless you count the banished one, so I didn't fear anyone trying to undermine me. On those days when I felt guilty, I perked myself up by going shopping.

Shopping became something I did all the time. Somehow it made the guilt seem lighter, at least for that moment when I was making a purchase. Looking back, I rarely bought anything for myself; it was always for my family. I see now that must have been the guilt too. I spent the money like it wouldn't be there tomorrow. I suppose that's why I spent it rather than saved it. If I ever got caught, they could take my last nickel away from me, but if I spent it first, then at least I'd had the pleasure of having had that experience. Surely they wouldn't confiscate *stuff*, but if I had a big chunk of change in a bank account somewhere, they might well have been able to get at that.

I did manage to save some money, as little as it was. I put it into my company's 401(k) plan, thinking that if I were ever found out, the government would protect me from losing it. And if not—well, I would simply have to fight that battle when the time came.

But by and large I managed to get through the rough times by shopping. It had become an addiction, something I did to ease the anxiety of life. I always shopped alone and was able to shut out everything else in my life when I was in a store. I only bought things I really liked, but I sought out these things as if they were a matter of life and death.

I made up shopping games in my head, challenging myself to find certain clothes or outfits, and went at these challenges with a vengeance. I spent many hours shopping, dropping thousands of dollars along the way. As I passed through the checkout line I didn't even hear the girl tell me how much the bill was; I simply signed the receipt and went on my way. I no longer had many credit cards, so the cash was sucked right out of our bank account. I never spent more than we had, but I spent money we should have been saving for a rainy day.

My workdays were mostly spent toward managing people, a task I found I enjoyed very much. I went on costly business trips and out on my boss's sixty-eight-foot yacht with the other people who worked for him. I had garnered respect, a great salary, a sports car, beautiful clothes, a Rolex watch, and everything else I had wanted in my twenties. Sometimes it was enough. Other times I felt like a fake and a phony and that I was in over my head.

I felt as if I was working too hard and neglecting my family. I felt as if my daughter was being raised by everyone but me. The daughter I had started this whole damned lie for to begin with. The daughter I didn't see for days at a time.

Here I was, making it in a man's world, worrying about woman's stuff. I had never seen a difference before, but I was starting to realize the varying expectations placed on women as opposed to men. We were expected not only to be mothers and take care of the family but also to bring home some bacon. Or was I placing that expectation on myself while the rest of the world thought I should just be spending more time at home? The daddies were expected to see their kids in the evening or whenever they were in town, but the mommies were supposed to be there 24/7. How was I supposed to find the time, with everything else that was going on in my life? Idealistic notions like working part-time or from home didn't click in the cutthroat world I lived in. I was faced with having to sacrifice one for the other. I made that choice every day.

None of my male counterparts seemed to have that problem—or at least none expressed it to me. Some of them even had wives who didn't work at all, so they got to be the heroes of the family who made enough money to provide for their families while keeping mommy safe and secure at home. They didn't experience the guilt for not being there because they weren't *expected* to be there. They were the men, out foraging for their families—they were doing what was expected of them as a parent. Many of the women at my level didn't even have kids. Was that the only time it was acceptable to be out here hitting it hard with the big boys? Was that the only excuse for acting like a man in corporate America?

Some people—especially other women—judged me. Sometimes I knew their opinions arose out of jealousy, but other times I felt they pitied me a little. I would be out of town on a business trip and someone would ask if I had any kids. I would tell them yes, I had a daughter, and they would ask if I had any pictures. The first time I was asked that, I realized I didn't have a single picture in my purse. I was horrified—and so was the lady who had asked me. She had pictures of her family that she showed off lovingly, and it made me stop to wonder how far out of touch with my family I had really become.

When I returned to my office, I looked around and noticed that the framed pictures I had of my daughter at work were outdated by a couple of years. I realized that I had never even seen her school pictures that year; her grandmother must have picked her up on the day they handed them out. My family never "bothered" me with that kind of thing because I was so busy. They allowed me simply to be me and to work outside the home, and they never told me how that made them feel. In a way, they enabled me. But I was such a "strong" person that I can't blame them. I have no doubt I lived up to every inch of my Ice Princess nickname.

Besides, even if they had complained, I would simply have swept it under the rug or bought them something to pacify them. Even though the needles of doubt were beginning to prick deeply, I couldn't tolerate hearing such things out loud—things that might make me doubt my mission even more. Everyone else could choose to either climb on board or be ridiculed for questioning my career. I didn't give them a whole lot of choices, but I was too busy to worry about things such as that.

I think back to those days now and brush tears from my eyes as I wonder at what point my daughter finally gave up on me. Or did she never even hope for anything more than what I had been for her? Had I been so wrapped up in my job for so long that she didn't even think it was strange that her grandmother took her to the dentist? Did she wonder why I never asked about her day? She knew the things that would get my attention, like her quarterly report card, and this drove her to get very good grades. Somehow I found the five minutes a quarter to gush over her report card, and I distinctly remember how she glowed at those times. I should have been making her glow every day. I should have been accessible all the time, but I wasn't.

If she called me at work, I rushed through our conversation. She never complained, because that's the only mother she knew. I have so much work to do to make up for those times. I did so much damage that can never be undone, and I am so afraid of what long-term problems that kind of distance between a mother and daughter might create.

There were times when I was impatient with her and felt terrible about it later. There were times when I vowed to myself that I would make more time to be with her. Sometimes I would be successful for a brief period, and then I would fall back into my routine and lose every inch of ground I had gained. The inconsistency I displayed was probably worse than simply not trying at all. I am sure my daughter felt hopeful time and again that I had changed—only to find that I hadn't.

As the years passed and my stress grew as a result of my increased responsibility at work, my level of impatience with anything that rocked my boat increased as well. I was quick to yell at my daughter if she was crabby or tired, even though I hadn't been there the night before to make sure she had gotten to bed on time. By enabling me, my family had created a need for them to accept that I was too busy to be bothered by mundane family activities. Too busy and tired and impatient—and certainly not in line for any Mother of the Year Award.

Once, at my daughter's birthday party, she and her girlfriend were arguing over a silly rubber ball and I kept telling them to relax and play with something else. My daughter was being unreasonable because it was her birthday, and her friend was being unreasonable because she was kind of a brat to begin with. They kept taking it from each other and bickering. I told them to stop several times, each time my impatience growing exponentially. After the third time, I went to the kitchen, grabbed a knife from the drawer, and stormed back into the room. I took the ball and stabbed it sharply. It made a loud POP and deflated into a shriveled piece of rubber.

The roomful of kids fell silent. All of the children looked at me with their eyes as big as saucers. The adults couldn't even look me in the eye. I stood there with the huge knife in one hand and the remains of the ball in the other. I said something stupid like "Okay let's get back to the party," and that was that.

Shortly after, everyone left.

More than a symbol of my discontent, the ball incident was a clear sign that something was wearing on me—something big. Something inside of me was eating away at the normal person who used to hang out in there. I had lost my composure in front of others. Thank God they hadn't been arguing over a hamster or something.

The incident made me feel as if I couldn't do anything that a mommy was supposed to do. I couldn't deal with bickering kids. I couldn't cope with schedules. I couldn't even clean my own house; I hired someone to do it for me. Each week I would return home to find everything clean. It seemed unreal to me and never stopped freaking me out. My family relished in this, and we became a bunch of slobs. Since Mommy was no longer going to yell about it, they had a free ticket to mess up anything they wanted to, especially on Tuesday, the day before the maids showed up.

My wifely performance in the bridal suite wasn't exactly winning me any awards, either. Besides being physically absent a lot of the time, I had more than adequate reasons for maintaining my title as Ice Princess. I was so busy and so tired all the time that I felt everything I did was justified by the amount of money I made. At least that's what I told myself. If my husband desired more intimacy, I'd buy him a new video game to play on a top-of-the-line entertainment system I had bought him the week before. If he wanted to talk about something he felt was important, I'd get him a new lawn mower. I did whatever it took to keep him busy, and in turn he grew accustomed to his wife being her ever-phony self. I never slowed down long enough to ask him if everything was okay. It wasn't that I didn't care; I just knew I couldn't take the time to do anything about it, so why bother even bringing it up?

One Christmas I got a clear picture of just how unloved my husband must have been feeling. I decided we should send holiday cards to my parents and enclose a DVD copy of the movie *National Lampoon's Christmas Vacation*. The movie was one I had watched in my younger years with my family and I thought my parents would enjoy it.

My husband, having the latest and greatest of everything, had a DVD burner and made two copies of the movie for me to enclose in my parents' cards. I wrote some sentimental messages inside each card and told them how much the movie reminded me of my own childhood.

A few days later, only a few days shy of Christmas, my mother telephoned me at work. She said that she had received my card and the movie, but she went on to say that she didn't think I had sent the correct movie. I asked what she meant, and she said, "Well, we [she and her boyfriend] are sitting here watching it and . . . well, let me just tell you the name of the movie . . ."

I was beginning to get irritated because I had no idea what she was talking about, but my heart began to sink as she went on. "The name of the movie is *Young Girls in Lust*, and right now there is a girl on a desk beginning to take her clothes off."

My mind was racing, trying to comprehend what she was saying. I could faintly hear some weird music in the background. It dawned on me that somehow my mother had received a pornographic movie inside of her Christmas card. I snapped to my senses and shouted at her to turn it off. I heard the music stop suddenly. I apologized profusely and told her that I didn't know how that happened. I was so embarrassed and ashamed.

Unfortunately, the horror didn't stop there. After all, I had sent the same DVD to my father and had not yet heard from him. My next move was to call my husband in hysterics, screaming at him about how he could possibly burn porn and have me send it to my parents.

He was apologetic and said he must have been drunk, but there was a possibility that my father may not have received the wrong movie. I clung to this hope, however remote it was. I could have called and told him not to watch the film, but that would only spark his curiosity. So I decided to wait and hope for the best.

A couple days later I got the call, and, sure enough, my father had received the porno too. He sounded as if he thought it were some kind of joke, and I appreciated that. I am certain he really thought that we must have a porno collection so large that we were unable to keep it separated from our holiday films.

I was devastated that my parents had experienced that during the holidays, but I was also devastated that my husband had a porno collection I knew nothing about. I had never asked if he watched such things, but I was certainly surprised to find out that he did. I was upset—all the more so because of what I perceived to be my own responsibility in the situation. I mean, what did I expect him to do? I wasn't giving him what he needed, so he used his high-tech toys to create some sort of substitute.

I realized he was suffering, but I was too angry about what happened to care. Or maybe I was too busy to care, and being angry became my excuse. One thing was clear—my Happy Pie was out of whack and I was the only one with the power to fix it.

# CHAPTER FOURTEEN

My health, both physical and mental, popped up on my internal radar in my thirties. Things I had never thought about before, let alone worried about, suddenly became pesky irritants that wouldn't let go, especially when I was trying to get some sleep. I don't remember when it started, but I began to fear getting sick and dying. Some nights I would lie awake and be terrified that maybe I had a brain tumor or breast cancer or something equally scary. I came to realize my days on this planet are not infinite, and I had no way of calculating how much time I had left.

Of course, like most people who experience such internal fears, I swore that I would begin eating better, getting more exercise, and visiting my doctor more regularly. But I avoided the doctor particularly because I realized that if he told me something was seriously wrong with me, I probably would have a mental breakdown right there in his office. The thought terrified me so much that I tried desperately to put it out of my mind.

There was a several-month period in which I had stomachaches so bad that I finally did go to the doctor. He examined me and suggested that I have a colonoscopy. I knew what this was because my father had had the pleasure of undergoing several throughout the years. I knew the doctor would thread some sort of scope up through my butt and look at everything inside of me to see what was out of whack.

He suspected I might have some polyps or something else but wanted to rule out anything really sinister. While not crazy about the idea, I scheduled the procedure a few weeks later and headed down to the medical center to have it done. I didn't realize at that time that I was going to have an IV and be put under twilight anesthesia. I found out only shortly before I went into the room for my test, and fear suddenly gripped me like a vise. I began to cry. I felt panic grip me. I refused to get out of my seat. The idea of being sedated to the point of being nearly unconscious struck me hard. The nurses tried to calm me down by telling me how routine it all was. I told them the procedure didn't scare me, but the anesthesia did. I had been under once before for surgery, but that had been an emergency situation and I had been barely conscious. I guess I had assumed they would numb me somehow, not knock me out. I would even have been happy with an epidural!

One of the nurses suggested that the doctor scheduled to do the procedure come out and talk to me. I thought that meeting him would ease my mind and that everything would be okay. At the very least, it would delay my trip back to the room to get my delirium injection.

The nurse went to get the doctor while I hung my head and cried. Here was the real me again, brought out by fear. I didn't care that everyone was staring at me or that I couldn't be brave. All I could think about was that I did not want to die that day.

The nurse came back with the doctor and I looked up to greet him. He was cross-eyed. I thought I was going to die right then and there. Was this their idea of a joke? *This* was the guy who was going to thread a scope up through my backside? I thought of those tricks we did as kids where we would shut one eye and try to put two pencils end to end, and they would turn out to be a foot and a half apart. How could this guy possibly thread something through my insides with any accuracy?

I began to shake and said that I needed to throw up. I went in the bathroom and tried, but since I had cleaned out my system the day before with all the pre-butt-scope procedures, nothing came up.

I came out of the bathroom and felt tired, worn down, ravaged. I hadn't eaten in a day and a half, and the fear was consuming every ounce of energy I had. I finally gave in out of sheer exhaustion and dragged myself back to the IV room. I don't remember much after that, but my procedure went okay.

Obviously outward appearances didn't have a lot to do with my doctor's ability to perform a colonoscopy. Well, except maybe for winning the patient's confidence during a panic attack.

I wondered if the doctor ended up doing this type of work because he usually never met the patients before they were sedated. Maybe he tried to be a regular doctor but no one could muster enough faith in him because he looked like a cartoon character. I'll never know, but I felt bad for him anyway.

Looking back, I'm glad I went through with the procedure, but I wish I hadn't gone to throw up after seeing that he was cross-eyed. He had to have seen the panic in my face go from bad to worse. I feel bad about that.

I know now that all of my new anxieties were partly a result of getting older, but I also think it was a symptom of stress. There were days when I was wound so tightly that I would suddenly realize I had been clenching my jaw for hours. When I made a conscious effort to relax, my teeth were sore from having been ground together. On the outside I appeared calm and cool, but on the inside I was buzzing. Things were building up inside of me, and I began having irrational fears. Because of the phony persona I had created for myself, I had to think through everything I said and did. I had to try harder and I had to be alert all the time. I was exhausting myself from the inside out. I was playacting my way through life. I was wearing costumes and being ON and going through the paces without missing a beat, but I was paying for it all with my mental well-being.

My phobias began, simply enough, with a fear of water. I had never been crazy about water or swimming, but I had never been afraid of it as a kid. I took swimming lessons when I was young, and, although I was no marathon swimmer, I could get by in the deep end of the pool. Suddenly, in my thirties, I began having nightmares about drowning in deep, dark water. My dreams became petrifying. I would see myself choking and gasping and unable to get a breath. At that point I would wake up shaking and sweating.

Then the dreams somehow began spilling over into real life and I started avoiding water. The mere thought of being in water up to my knees made my skin crawl. I knew the water in the dreams probably didn't represent real water, but that didn't stop real water from making me queasy.

The phobia grew so strong that simply taking a bath sent my heart racing with fear. I felt like the water was closing in on me and would crush me from all sides. I knew in my mind it couldn't, but somehow I couldn't stop the fear.

I didn't know it then, but that was the beginning of a series of real panic attacks that would begin to plague me for the next several years. Stress was closing in on me, but I was clueless as to its approach. If anyone had asked me, I would have told him I was "one of the luckiest people alive, loving life, fantastic." But something was happening inside of me that I couldn't control—something I couldn't smother or simply put out of my mind anymore. Something was continuing to bubble up inside of me, and I didn't even know it.

Maybe in college I would have learned more about the conscious and subconscious minds, but I had no clue that my subconscious mind could have any effect on what happened to my body in real life. I was, in a sense, being eaten from the inside out, and I didn't have a clue why. Things were happening inside of me that I was unaware were happening.

After the colonoscopy incident I was too afraid to see a doctor, and I refused to believe it could be stress. I looked around at my life and saw all the material things I had. Those things plus the respect and the solid career I had going for me made me feel like an idiot. I was living my idea of the Great American Dream: I could pay my bills, I lived life large, and other people envied me. How could I want to be happier? How could I be stressed out? The notion that something as unimportant as my subconscious could put a damper on my health seemed ridiculous. I had made a career out of burying silly thoughts like that, but suddenly I could no longer keep them under control.

Little phobias continued to pop up—extreme fear of bugs, walking inside gas stations, taking any kind of medicine, and driving over bridges, just to name a few. I guess they were a form of mental illness brought on by stress.

Sometimes I had panic attacks out of the blue. I would be sitting in my office and my heart would begin to race. In my panic, I thought I was dying and lived through twenty minutes of hell until it ended with me regurgitating in the bathroom. When my attacks became more frequent, I knew something was wrong, but I couldn't decide how to deal with them because they would only return.

To make matters worse, I also began feeling all those normal aches and pains that accompany aging. Every time I felt a sore muscle in my back I panicked, thinking I was having a heart attack. A shooting pain in my head had to be a stroke. It never occurred to me in the midst of an attack how ridiculous the panic was. I was so afraid of dying that anything that put me at risk or felt like something was wrong sent me over the edge. I drove more slowly, ate better, and bought a new security system for my house.

My lack of faith came to play a large role in my phobias too. I actually feel cheated when it comes to religion. I am certain I must be missing some fundamental quality that the majority of other people have. I would give *anything* to believe in my heart of hearts that so long as I am a good person I will go to this great place called heaven when I die. If I could flip a switch and be a believer, I would do it in a second. I envy those people who appear to believe beyond a shadow of a doubt in God or Buddha or whomever. Some of them may look a little crazy at times, but I think my life would be so much easier if that question of life after death were answered in my mind.

Am I cursed with some terrible extra layer of logic that blocks me from being able to believe in a concept such as heaven? If I could somehow make myself believe, it would be a weight lifted off my shoulders. Life would be easier to bear, and my stress would be considerably lessened.

I have doubts, though, and therefore I can't be a believer. If I said I believed, I would just be lying, and all lying would do is make me appear more politically correct. It wouldn't do anything to help me become less fearful of dying.

As it stands, I fear that we simply expire when we die. Kind of like when we go to sleep, but without the waking up part. That's it, you're done. Just writing those words puts a lump of fear in my throat. I don't want to believe that, but I do. And I cannot figure out how other people do it. I sometimes wonder if they really do, or if they just say they do but have that same shadow of doubt deep inside. Why do I need proof? Why can't I just sleep well at night knowing it is all taken care of? What is wrong with me?

Sometimes I get angry at the all those religious people I see on TV. I like to blame them for making religion look so ridiculous, like some giant moneymaking scheme contrived to make people think that religion is anything but human-made. But the fact remains that short of witnessing Noah and his ark sailing through downtown Seattle to rescue me and my family from the Flood, I don't believe it. *I don't know how to believe it.*

I cannot talk myself into blind faith. That merely feeds my fears of dying. The fears appeared in my thirties and compounded the stress I was already feeling. I even began to fear my stress! I knew from things I read that stress can be a silent killer. I also knew that the jaw stiffness and periodic tightness in my chest were bad signs that I was suffering on the inside. The panic attacks were also an undeniable symptom of stress. But I was unable to stop it—the stress was simply beyond my ability to stop. I wanted to live as long as possible. I wanted my one ride on the whirly-whirl to count.

Worst of all, I didn't know the most terrifying day of my life was upon me.

# CHAPTER FIFTEEN

Flying—I did it all the time. I flew to different places around the country for work at least four times a month. I enjoyed flying because it gave me time to work without being bothered. Sometimes I would just read magazines or books, which is something I never had time to do when I was home.

I had never flown in a plane until I was nineteen years old, so I was fascinated by it at first, and then just looked at it as a pleasant break in my schedule. I didn't even mind the airports too much. I was able to eat and get a coffee while I waited, and I always felt very professional, all dressed up while waiting for my plane: the perfect likeness of everything I always wanted to be.

And then, one night, I found myself sitting in the airport in Miami waiting for a plane that had been delayed in the Keys. It was an hour late and arrived close to midnight. I was tired and planned to read a magazine on the short flight home.

The plane was a nineteen-seat Piece-of-Crap, the oldest-looking plane I had ever been on. We boarded from the tarmac, which wasn't out of the ordinary, but unfortunately it gave me a good look at the thing. For the first time in my life, I felt a twinge of fear while getting on a flight. My seat was in the last row, which had three seats but only one other passenger. The other rows had only two seats, one on each side of the center aisle. I sat on the left side of the plane with the empty seat between myself and the other lady in my row.

When everyone was finally seated, the pilot and copilot climbed aboard. The pilot came back to the cabin and announced that the plane's intercom system was malfunctioning, and since the plane was too small for any additional crew, there would be no communication between us and them until we landed. He said we would hear a recorded fasten seatbelts warning just before landing, but other than that we were on our own. That was fine by me, and I settled in to read my magazine. The takeoff went smoothly, and we were soon airborne.

Now, I had been on several flights that experienced turbulence, but I wasn't ready for what was about to happen. Only ten minutes into the flight we entered stormy skies. Our first indication that something was wrong was a sudden drop in altitude. The plane dipped so hard and fast that anyone who had unbuckled his seatbelt hit the ceiling. I could see everything from where I was seated and couldn't believe my eyes. People screamed and appeared to be hurt—and then the lights went out. There was more screaming and the plane dropped several more times.

When the plane wasn't dropping, it was banking hard from side to side. It felt as if the pilot was literally trying to wrest control of the plane back from God.

My eyes gradually adjusted to the dark and I remember seeing the man in the row in front of me in the crash position—head down between his legs. I shut my eyes and tried to block it out, but the nightmare continued. I heard the woman next to me crying and praying, and I realized that everyone else on the plane thought the same thing I did: We were going down and we were all going to die. I began to hyperventilate and couldn't stop. I still had my magazine in my hand, and when I opened my eyes to try to focus on it, I saw that I was shaking so hard that the magazine was just waving back and forth in front of me like I was fanning myself. I couldn't breathe, and I couldn't stop the fear that swept over me. It wasn't a panic attack; it was a real life-and-death situation that had engulfed us all.

Suddenly, a man a few rows up started yelling at me, "Hey you!" I couldn't speak, but I looked at him as he continued on. "Look out your window and tell us if we're going down!" I couldn't understand at the time what he was talking about, and then I realized that the plane was so small that only the people in the very back could see out the windows around the wings. He wanted to know if we were about to slam into the ground.

He yelled at me again, but I couldn't move. I couldn't bring myself to look out. If I had seen the ground closing in, I would have died before impact of sheer horror. He was scared, too, and became angry that I was doing nothing. I finally screamed back that I wasn't going to look out the window and for him to shut up and turn back around. He blinked, as if I had just slapped him in the face, and slowly turned back around and sat down.

For that brief moment the real me had surfaced. It was a flash of desperation that surprised even me. Apparently, when faced with death I still existed and could bubble to the surface if I had to.

As unpleasant as the flight was, I began climbing out of my panic. I caught my breath, and my flow of thoughts slowly returned. I thought about my daughter and my dogs and I hoped that they knew how much I loved them. I thought of my parents and I thought of how desperately I wanted to live. I couldn't even call them on my cell phone to tell them goodbye because my purse was lost somewhere, rattling around the plane with the rest of the luggage.

In those few moments of mental clarity, I also thought about my lie. I thought that people whom I had never met would come to my funeral, compare notes, and realize that I had no degree. It was such a trivial thought compared to dying, but it was as real as anything I've ever thought in my life.

Was this the ultimate payback for deceiving people and spending all that money I earned based on my false foundation? Was this a plane full of bad people on our doomed trip to Blink-Out City? Had everyone on board committed some victimless crime and the joke was now on us?

Suddenly the lights came on. We were still dropping every few minutes and banking pretty hard, but I could swear it seemed a little better. I knew it could be my mind telling me that so I didn't slip over the edge into insanity, but it worked. We had been slammed around for more than twenty minutes, and my adrenaline must have been running low. I was able to rationalize that if we were going to crash, it would have happened by now.

The other people on the plane were starting to calm down too. No one was screaming, although a lot of people were still crying and clutching each other. I was still shaking, but less so by the moment. I made a promise to myself that I would never fly again if I could just make it safely to the ground.

Slowly but surely the turbulence subsided and I felt the plane level out and begin a controlled decent. I finally worked up the courage to look out the window and recognized the lights that were my city. The recorded seatbelt message came on, and I had never been so happy to hear it in all my life.

When the plane landed, everyone cheered. Afterward, the pilot came into the cabin and tried to make light of what had happened. He asked who on board was never going to fly again. Everyone was too shaken up to respond, but I'm betting most of the people wanted to shout out, "Me!"

I got off the plane weak and exhausted. I ended up sitting in the airport for an hour, unable to walk. I sat and cried with my face in my hands. I was so grateful to be there and so grateful not to have died that night. I was eventually able to get my car from the lot and drive home. I told my husband what had happened and he tried to comfort me.

Afterward, I realized that I could very easily have died that night, and I never wanted to feel that way again. That night I added one more thing to my list of phobias: fear of flying.

All of my phobias up until then had been minor inconveniences. They had rarely interfered with my life, let alone my job. I didn't like water, so I didn't go swimming. I didn't like gas stations, so I paid at the pump. I hated bugs, so I enlisted someone else to squash them.

Now I hated flying. I was terrified to do something I was expected to do several times a month. I had promised myself I wouldn't fly again, but I already had two flights booked within the next two weeks. I was going to have to renege on that promise. Somehow.

I told myself I would relax and it would get easier. I had long heard that getting back into the saddle after being thrown from your horse is the best medicine. Maybe I just had to saddle up soon and everything would be all right.

I had convinced myself that bigger planes would be fine. So when it came time to board a large plane for a flight to Tallahassee, I was anxious but confident—until I began that long, last walk. With every step I took, I felt panic nipping at my heels. What's more, the thought of going into a panic made me panic all the more. I was almost as afraid of having a full-blown attack on the plane as I was of crashing.

Once settled aboard, I concentrated on the task at hand: mind over matter, after all. But by the time we took off, I was a wreck. When the pilot retracted the plane's landing gear, I was sure we were going to crash. I never before noticed so much noise coming from the belly of the cabin. When the noise finally stopped, the man sitting next to me looked over and said jokingly, "Sounds like the wheels just fell off."

That was it. That was all it took. My heart racing, my knuckles white from their grip on the arm rests, I promised myself this would be it. No more flying. Ever. No matter what!

Even though the rest of the flight—and my day's work at my remote office—went well, when it came time to return home, I cashed in my ticket and rented a car. I had never before been so happy to spend four hours behind the wheel!

After that flight, reality started to set in that I was a jet-setting executive who had become afraid of jets. The mere thought of boarding a plane made my stomach turn. I canceled all pending air travel and told myself I would figure it out later. Surely there had to be some way around the problem, some shortcut I could take that would keep me from going aerial again. There had to be a way that nobody would get hurt—especially me.

Finally, the time came when I realized I wasn't going to be able to solve this problem myself, so I decided to consult a psychiatrist. Ever since the tragedy of 9/11, there must have been plenty of people dealing with the same fear of flying. I felt better knowing I wasn't alone.

I had to wait a month to see the only doctor covered by my health plan who handled flying fears, and I was anxious to do whatever he had in store to get my phobia behind me. I was hoping he could hypnotize me or something equally quick and make the nightmare go away.

I showed up for my appointment and started filling out the preliminary paperwork. When I finally finished up and went into the doctor's office, I was pleasantly surprised. He was a well-dressed guy with a smug attitude, but at least he inspired some confidence. He asked me what I was there to see him about and I explained that I had a fear of flying, among other things, and I needed his help to make it go away. I started into my story of how I believed I acquired my fear, but he cut me short. He began writing on a piece of paper, and I asked him what he was doing. "Prescribing some Xanax," he said. I sat there, a little confused, before I politely told him that I would rather talk my way past my problem than have to rely on drugs.

He laughed and said that he was a psychiatrist, not a psychologist. Besides, he insisted that my particular phobia would be easier to treat with drugs.

I finally took the prescription—and got him to recommend a psychologist. A few weeks later, I visited the man and was surprised at the condition of his office. It was damp and old, and the furniture looked as if it had been there forever. On the day of my appointment, the secretary's dog was having puppies and they apparently thought it was fine that she have them right there in the office. I watched for a little while before I was called in.

The therapist was nice enough, and, after listening to my story, he used a lot of big words to tell me that I was suffering from post-traumatic stress disorder brought about by the bad flight I had experienced. I was hoping he would tell me something I didn't know.

In the end, he advised me to go to the airport and watch the planes coming and going for several days in a row. That, he said, would help my conscious mind get through to my subconscious mind the fact that flying wasn't so dangerous after all.

It all sounded too simple to me. I couldn't understand how simply watching planes take off and land was going to cure me, but I gave it my best shot—and, sure enough, I'd been right. I was even more anxious about flying after a week's worth of observation than I had been before.

So when my firm held a huge meeting in Las Vegas that I had to attend, I had my prescription for Xanax filled and took half a milligram. As takeoff time approached, I felt the need for another half . . . and then another, and, finally, a fourth, bringing the total up to two full milligrams.

The drugs helped me through the flight—as well as the return flight home—although I recall vaguely having made a complete idiot of myself in front of my CEO and several other people from work. But in the end, all was forgiven: I'd done my job, and I looked forward to flying never again.

# CHAPTER SIXTEEN

As the weeks passed, I noticed that my traumatic experience with flying had left yet one more fear—one that was totally new to me. For the first time in my life, I began to fear being away from my family.

I had always loved my parents, as well as my daughter, but somehow loving was no longer enough. I realized that I had been so frightened on that fateful flight because I thought I was going to die. I didn't want to die because I had too much to live for. I wasn't ready to go out like that. And the thought of dying made every important person in my life that much more important. I wanted to grab them and hold them and be near them. I felt anxious every time I was away from home.

My daughter, who up until then saw me twice a week at most, became the only thing I could think about. What if she fell off her bike and I was five hundred miles away? What if she woke up from a nightmare and I wasn't there to comfort her? What if she died on Friday and I hadn't seen her since Tuesday? I felt as if I had to be present everywhere my loved ones were in order to control everything that happened to them. I felt that if I were there, nothing would go wrong.

My new resolution never to fly again didn't help matters any. As an alternative, I began to drive everywhere I had to go. Some of my destinations were six hours away. All that time in the car not only kept me from being with my family even more, but it also gave me way too much time to think—to worry—to wonder. And I covered all the bases—my daughter, my husband, my parents, even my dogs.

I worried about myself too. Mostly I worried that I would die young and no longer be available to my family. My guilt from all those years away had turned into anxiety, and it was becoming severe. I was beginning to resent corporate America and beginning to shy away from my own job. I sat through meetings, disgusted with myself and everyone else in the room for what we seemed to represent. We were cogs in the giant Wheel of Industry and Finance. We deserted our families and spouses day after day and never looked back. Our kids were spoiled and overweight and being raised by someone else.

Yet the others just sat through the meetings, content to find new ways to compete with one another. Their passion was their work, and it was all most of them ever cared about—much like someone else I could name, if I absolutely had to.

Don't get me wrong: I knew that many people have to work, and I knew that there are plenty of folks who want nothing more than to be home with their families. I was just as sure that, the bigger the big shot, the less likely he or she cared at all. In upper management, self-worth is based upon what other people at work think about you and how much money you bring home each week. I had been one of these people myself. Now I felt as if I were awakening from a bad dream. I felt as if I wanted to run away from all those "other" kinds of people, to yell out that I was no longer one of them. Sitting there listening to them argue for hours about which department should get which office space made me want to vomit. I wanted to slap every one of them and ask them where their priorities were. Who cares about such things? Who really cares?

And then I thought, *Well . . . I had cared*. A year before I would have cared a lot. I would have put more than two cents into any conversation where people would listen to me. Now all I did was sit back and try to salve my aching head as the discussions droned on and on . . .

The lessons I had learned early in life about corporations being nothing more than machines kept haunting me. I had become another player in the game. I told people things to keep them performing as good employees, as good cogs in the machine. I had given people advice about their lives based on what was best for my company—and for me. I had become one of those figureheads who look at everything based on personal and corporate gain. My own decisions had been based on this contrived image of what someone in my position would look, act, and be like. I had aspired to become something I didn't even like. And the worst part is that I had seen evidence of that long before I arrived at where I was. I was only another rat in the race. That was all I had become, and the clothes, shoes, and perfume were not able to cover up the reality that I was nothing more than a rat.

I looked at the goals I had set professionally for myself and saw that they weren't *my* goals, but instead they were my company's goals. Where were my *personal* goals, and did I even have any?

I feared that somewhere along the way, I had lost myself as a person, a mother, a wife, and a friend. I had lost it all because I was too busy trying to be a cog in the machine. I was trying to impress people who couldn't have cared less whether or not I was happy or sad so long as I did a great job. And to top it off, they cared only that I did a great job because that would reflect well on them—because their bosses in turn would think *they* did a great job. It was a catch-22, and I had been caught right in the middle.

It was nobody's fault. We were all doing what we were expected to do, and we had been brainwashed into thinking that it made us important. Truthfully, it made us forgettable and ordinary. The fact was that we weren't out saving the world or doing anything to be proud of. We were a little piece of a larger machine that was a little piece of a larger machine and so forth on up the line, and those machines didn't care what happened in our lives. If they said they cared about our happiness, it was only because being happy made us more productive. That wasn't true caring; it was the machine in disguise.

For the first time in my life I started skipping work. I didn't want to go. I wanted to stay home and do nothing. I would sit home by myself and drink coffee. I didn't turn on the TV or talk on the phone. I sat in silence in my house and wished a hundred times I could sit there forever. Yet the days went by so quickly. I craved picking my daughter up from school. I would look forward to it all day long and be the first parent there after school. Then would come a kick in the teeth: My daughter would get in the car and, in her innocence, ask why I was there to pick her up. Sometimes she actually seemed disappointed. I'm sure she must have had something fun planned with her grandma, and I had ruined it. Kids are like that, I know, but it still hurt me deeply. I had let too much time go by, and now I felt like an intruder in my own family's life.

Those feelings kept coming and kept getting worse. I no longer worried about getting found out at work; in fact, I began to wish I would. It might be horrible for a few days, but it would end the meaningless effort I was forced to put forth every day of my life.

At work, I went from overcompensating for my shortcomings to barely caring. I was rude, fed up, and unimpressed with anyone. I was bitter about how much of my life I had wasted trying to be like these people. If someone told me she was thinking about leaving the firm, I told her to go ahead. Who cares?

I feel bad about that now. Those people didn't know my internal struggles, and some of them really relied on me for my opinions. I wanted to hurt the company for what I felt it had taken from me. I had no one else to blame it on except this entity—this monstrous *thing* that I couldn't see or touch but could only resent and blame. I wanted it to crumble so that all of my co-workers could go home to their families. I know that sounds ridiculous, but I had already mentally checked out of the career that just kept going—like the Energizer Bunny—seemingly forever.

# CHAPTER SEVENTEEN

Let me take a step back and tell you about my parents and their role in my life. As with everything else, I have only recently come to realize their importance in the choices that I have made throughout my career.

From the beginning, my mother pushed me to be successful and my father pushed me to be happy. If only I had listened to both of them. My love for my father is immeasurable and reciprocal. He was hard on me only when I deserved it, and otherwise let me make my own mistakes.

My mother was a little tougher on me emotionally. She wanted me to be *somebody*, because she never was. I knew as I was growing up that she wanted me to be successful, but I never knew why.

I was a brilliant child, and my mother pinned her hopes on me as the brain of the family, while my sister was destined to be the beauty.

Once, in my early teens, while I was watching television with my mother, she told me that I wouldn't enjoy being a model like the women on TV because they have to shave their legs twice a day to stay perfect for all their photo shoots. I told her that didn't sound very difficult, so she told me that my legs were too short, anyway. She said I had my dad's legs. I remember looking at myself objectively in the mirror for the first time that day. I had never known I had short legs, but I figured I must—why else would my mother point that out?

Well *now* I know she pointed it out because she wanted me to be *somebody*—not just a pretty face, but somebody smart and successful who didn't rely on her beauty, as she had, to get through life. She made me feel ugly to save me from ending up where "pretty" had gotten her.

My mother didn't let me wear makeup for a long time and always permed my hair at home, each time turning out worse than the last. My hair was naturally curly anyway, so it escaped me why she would want to make me over to look like Ronald McDonald. I know now that it was to help keep me ugly so that I could be successful because I was smart.

Unfortunately for my mother, I blossomed in my late teens and became someone who, while not textbook beautiful, was able to attract boys without fail. My sister always was—and still is—more beautiful than I. The difference is that she always knew she was pretty, and I never did. I never thought my looks would get me anywhere—and I am thankful for that. My sister has suffered greatly for being raised as the "pretty child." She doesn't know any other way to get what she wants. The kicker is that she is also smart. She finished all but twenty credits toward her bachelor's degree before her son died. She never finished school or relied on her brains to see her through life again. She is still trying to wade through the pain of everything that happened more ten years ago. She is a very beautiful but very unhappy lady a lot of the time.

Her story is another book in itself, but the part it plays in mine is that my mother chose what *she* wanted us to be. I think both of us tried very hard to live up to what our mother's dreams were. My mother never finished high school but is one of the most persuasive people I know. She knows how to charm, when to insult, and just what to say to make her point. I think she used this ability on us to make us what she thought best for our lives.

Of course, someone that persuasive would be remiss if she didn't take her skills and spread them around. She practiced them on my father as well as on her daughters. He is very much like me in that we both take any kind of negative feedback as a challenge, so we were always attempting to improve ourselves in order to impress my mother.

I don't mean to make her sound manipulative, because that would imply that she didn't want what was best for us, and that would be untrue. She wanted us to be ideal—perfect reflections of what she would have been if given a second chance in life.

My mother knew my love of art and animals from a very young age. She discouraged me from either pursuit and encouraged me, instead, to develop my math and English skills so that I could grow up and make money. She knew I had the potential, and the fact remains that she was obviously correct, but my true passions were swept under the rug in favor of making me the smartest and most financially successful person I could be.

I won spelling bees and scored higher than anyone my age on state math exams, which made my mother proud. I did it all without effort, without studying.

My sister was doing it too, but for some reason it was less important to her than her wardrobe was. It was as if my mother wanted me to be a doctor and my sister to marry one. Maybe she just wanted to see which scenario played out better.

Any early successes I had toward achieving my mother's goals were rewarded and any deviations were criticized. I wanted to please her because doing so was a challenge, and so it went. If I wanted her to brag about me at the dinner table, I had to keep my drive going in the right direction.

My father mostly sat back and agreed with whatever pleased my mother. When I was young, all he ever said is that I could be whatever I wanted to be when I grew up. He did, however, encourage my art lessons and love of animals. He brought home stray dogs, much to my mother's dismay, and handed them to me to care for. I loved those dogs with all my heart and was sometimes allowed to keep them.

One dog in particular was a starved stray chocolate miniature poodle.

The dog was so sick it couldn't walk. A fireman friend of my father had found the dog lying in the road. My dad brought the dog home, and I nursed it, feeding it through a straw and dripping water on its tongue, for three days straight. I had never felt love such as I felt for that poor little dog. I named him and was allowed to keep him. Over the years my mother grew to hate that dog. I think she hated what he represented— a distraction from my schoolwork, and therefore from her goals.

Somehow, I believe that my father sensed my need to nurture that dog. It was his way of contributing, his way of keeping me alive inside. He knew there were pieces of me that were not being addressed in my life, either at school or at home. He knew that dog would keep my passion for animals alive inside of me, and I know he enjoyed seeing me light up every time I saw the dog.

In a lot of ways, my dad is kind of a tough guy, and he would never admit to having done so, but I can see it for what it was and will be forever grateful. He had the same burden I did: trying to please my mother, and the dog took a toll on that too. As I got older, especially into my twenties, my father became more vocal about what he thought. I guess with both kids out of the nest he too began to realize that life is short. That's when he started telling me about the one trip around the whirly-whirl and how I should make the most of it. He tolerated my mother's expectations less and less, and she became more and more unhappy with him.

After thirty-six years of marriage, my parents finally got divorced. By that time I lived out of state and got the news during a telephone call from my father. I had known they weren't getting along for many years, but I never thought they would split up. I was entering my thirties and it was just one more lesson learned.

My dad was devastated. My mother had left him for another man and taken half of Dad's 401(k) with her. All those years he had spent trying to please her had culminated in nothing. He was sixty years old and all alone. He was bitter and inconsolable. He felt cheated, as if he had wasted his life on something that didn't matter.

It made me so sad to talk to him that I avoided him most of the time. The man who had spent his life doing what was expected of him was paying the price. I'm not saying he had been the perfect husband; I am certain he was a pain in the butt most of the time. But he was a good man who loved his wife and children, and I always thought he deserved better. He worked hard for forty years so she wouldn't have to, but none of that mattered. I wished she had left him earlier. I don't think it would have hurt him any less, but at least he would have had more of his life left to recover from the pain. He had planned to retire later that year, but, after losing half his savings, he had to postpone that. Eventually, he retired with a fraction of what he had originally saved.

In my parents, I saw what happened to a marriage that wasn't nurtured through the years. Both of them had been playing roles and ignoring what they were feeling for much of their lives. Having the kids at home helped keep a sense of family intact, but once we flew the nest, their days were numbered.

They weren't living their own lives. My father was living the life my mother expected, and my mother was living vicariously through my sister and me, with little or no regard for my father at all. There was no passion. I can ask myself what I am passionate about in life and know what the answer will be. I don't know what either one of my parents is passionate about. How sad is that?

They got up every morning for decades to go do something they were not passionate about. They woke up each morning and made a choice to keep on faking it. And for years their reasons were good enough—stay together for the kids, she's a good mother, he's a good father—but once the reasons stopped making sense, there was nothing left to justify the lies. My parents had run out of excuses once too often, and suddenly none of it made any sense anymore. Unfortunately for them, they were thirty-six years into something that hadn't made sense. And thirty-six years is a long time to recuperate from.

I don't want to end up like that. I don't want to waste my life pretending to be something I am not, especially when it doesn't feel right anymore, with my boat, filled with all of my rationales and my reasons for being, beginning to leak. My father was right. We get only one trip around the whirly-whirl, and that's it. Game over. The only thing left behind after that is the memory of who we were and what we meant to those we leave behind. Did I want to be remembered more by the people I worked with or by my own daughter? The question seems easy enough to answer now, but back then, I just wasn't sure.

So my parents got a divorce and finally learned who they, themselves, were. At least I think that's what they learned. Today, my father seems relatively the same, although he laughs a little more easily and takes better care of himself than he used to when he was married.

My mother, on the other hand, has morphed into a person I hardly recognize. Her southern drawl, which she had abandoned decades ago, came creeping back, and she lives in a trailer. She is currently dating the "toughest man in town" in a one-stoplight community in the mountains near Nowhereville. He calls her "woman" and they gamble at cheesy casinos.

I speak to her on the phone occasionally, and I feel uneasy when I realize how much she helped shape my choices and pathways in life. Was she even aware she was doing it, or had she been trying to be the mother she thought everyone believed she should be? Had she really wanted to tell me to follow my heart and forget school and money and all the finer things in life? Had her advice been phony because she gave it when she was a phony? Or had her advice been intended to give me my independence because she never had hers? Either way, her words seemed suddenly contrived and misguided. My *real* mother apparently thought corporate America was a big waste of time and spent hours in her garden and ate beans and cornbread every night without worrying about where the next meal might come from. That's the mother I never knew.

For years she had bragged about me to her rather large extended family. She bragged that I was the first and one of the only kids in the family to graduate from college. I had led her to believe, after I moved to Florida, that I had gone back and finished school. She always pestered me about it, so I "did it." The long physical distance between us made the subterfuge easy.

She never asked about coming to my graduation (she didn't like to fly any more than I did) and I didn't make a big deal of it, for obvious reasons. I always wondered what my father thought when she said I had graduated, but I figured maybe he was never listening when she said it. He would have known better anyway—but maybe he knew why I lied to her and forgave me a little for that reason. After all, he wanted me to be happy.

My mother drinks during the day now, which is new, and doesn't have health insurance, which is also new. I worry about her a lot, but I also kind of envy her. She gave up everything she had, shocked everyone she knew, and set out to live her life the way she wanted to— and probably had wanted to for years. That took a lot of courage, no matter what anyone says about her. I would never ask her, but I am guessing she wishes she did it years ago. Time wasted trying to be some blurred version of yourself is just that—time wasted. Her excuses for being married and living behind the white picket fence ran out and she made a choice to stop pretending. I forgave her instantly for that, even after seeing my father's grief. She told me shortly after the divorce that she never felt as if she belonged in the family when she was with my father and his clan. She said she never felt good enough. I am guessing that she just never felt like herself. The fact remains that *this* is her trip around the whirly-whirl, and only she can make sure it's as good as it can be.

But I wonder. Had my mother figured out she wanted to live her life her way thirty years ago, would it have been any less devastating to those who knew her? Would my father have been hurt any less? I think he would have been hurt more emotionally back then, but less financially. Time was a tradeoff for less pain, but the time is gone either way, and they can't get it back.

It also makes me wonder how many people live their lives lying and faking and being phony for the greater good? What about the closeted lesbian? What about the wife who pretends to have a headache at night but goes out the next morning and lavishes herself in luxury? What about the bully who really only feels pain inside? What about all those people in love with someone other than the person they are with? All these people are phonies, and all of them are at risk of being found out. All of them are purposely living some life they don't even want. They are all doing it based on what is expected of them and what helps keep their balls in the air.

All of their reasons make sense for a while, and by the time their boats start to sink it seems too late—the water is too deep and it's too far from shore to swim. They think of everyone else's ride on the whirly-whirl, but not their own. How many people leave this world as someone they are not? How many people are remembered by loved ones who didn't even really know them?

I don't want to live in a trailer, and I don't like to grow my own tomatoes. I don't want to be poor. What I really wanted was the paycheck I was making plus more time at home. I wanted everyone to know that I was a born leader and not someone who had been finely crafted by higher education. I wanted to get the monkey off my back and let the world know who I really was.

Unfortunately, my life wasn't some romantic comedy where I came clean in desperation during some well-worded speech at the podium and everyone rallied around me because it was so touching. My life as I knew it hung in the balance of my next move. How could I go about becoming myself without destroying everyone and everything I loved in the process?

# CHAPTER EIGHTEEN

I wondered at times whether or not, had I gone to school and majored in business, as I said I had, I would have figured out that corporate life wasn't for me. I wondered about that often. But the wondering was soon replaced by the guilt of my success based upon false pretenses. I didn't know which was worse at the time, but I was about to find out.

In March 2005, news filtered throughout the corporation that unethical activities had been discovered. I immediately saw the lights fall on me. Soon enough, though, I learned the truth. My boss had been accused of embezzling more than $36 million from the company. Needless to say, an investigation was launched. And all hell was about to break loose.

My boss was supposed to be a decent guy—that's how he portrayed himself, and that's pretty much how everyone else saw him. He had worked at the firm for twenty years and had worked his way up from the bottom. He had a master's degree in taxation and was a bona fide CPA. He went through many years of school and had worked his butt off to get where he was. He was the CFO of a thirty-five-hundred-person firm with an impeccable reputation in the industry.

Above that, he had vision. He understood what was coming next and understood how to make employees happy. He was active in company efforts to make the firm a great place to work. He had skills that went far beyond basic Business 101: He understood people on a very personal basis. He was fun to be around, but he could be a very formidable opponent when challenged. He appeared to have his heart and soul planted firmly at work.

He was also rich. A-list movie star rich. He of course made a great salary at work, but his real riches came from his wife's side of the family—or so he claimed. He owned several mansions and a sixty-eight-foot yacht he used for company outings. He had a car collection that included a Ferrari, an Aston Martin, several Porsches, and too many others to name. He owned artwork you'd expect to see only in museums, and his two kids went to schools where nearly all the children were watched over not by nannies but by bodyguards.

I heard someone ask him once why he worked so hard if he had so much money, and he said he loved his work and it was the one thing he felt he did well and had a passion for. I was impressed, but looking back I see now that his answer made no sense at all—it wasn't like we were saving the world or curing cancer—but it sounded like a noble response at the time. The fact is that he was skimming money off the top of the books and hid it from everyone for more than fifteen years. The stories he told about his wife's family must have been untrue, or at least greatly exaggerated. I was on his yacht once on a company outing, and we were sitting at the table together when he told a story of how his wife's family dealt in international diamonds. He said they were so wealthy that as a child she used to play with bags of diamonds like they were bags of marbles. It was an impressive story, and certainly it would have explained the yacht and the case of thousand-dollar bottles of wine that the group had consumed in less than an hour the night before. I took everything he said at face value.

He spared no expense on our business trips. Our group of eight spent three days every six months yachting, meeting, drinking, and eating like royalty. We sailed to locations where only movie stars lived and drove golf carts that cost more than my real car. He let us drive his Ferrari and other sports cars as if they meant nothing to him. We nicknamed our group the Rockstars and partied like we were just that. I made a good friend during those trips, my counterpart in another state. She and I seemed kindred spirits, and we realized how odd these trips were but decided to enjoy them while we could. We had the same rebellious attitude and liked to hang out and babble like teenagers. Once, we shared a small room with two beds on the yacht. Our first night we were kept awake by the bilge pump sending off a warning beep every minute or so. We were pretty tired and had gone to bed earlier than everyone else that night because she had gotten seasick during the day.

Our bedroom was down a small flight of stairs, through a short hallway. There were two more bedrooms off the same hallway, one on either side of ours. About an hour after we turned in, we heard some other people come stumbling down the stairs just outside our door. We were lying in the dark—both awake—and could distinctly hear giggling: a man and a woman. I could make out the voice of one of my other counterparts . . . and my boss. They were giggling and talking and we heard her say, "No, not here," followed by the thud of their bodies hitting the wall and then what sounded like sloppy kissing. We both sat up in bed and looked at each other. She slowly got out of bed and peeked around the corner. She brought her head back in the room, and in the dim light I could see in her eyes the answer to my question. My boss was seducing one of his employees. Worse than that, although we thought the incident rather funny at first, we soon saw the darker side to the story. The woman was our direct corporate competition, and if she became involved with the boss, she would have a clear and dangerous advantage over us in the future.

I remember being amazed at how reckless they were. They *had* to know that we were only around the corner. I know that a lot of alcohol had been flowing that night, but wow! I wondered if that night was their first encounter or if it was merely one in a long number that had been going on for ages. I would have bet on that! The kicker is that the woman was actually great at her job. She worked hard and had accomplished things in her district that surpassed my own feats. Her kissing the boss in order to get ahead didn't make sense. Could there have been another reason? Perhaps she was eager to know if she still "had it." Maybe he was anxious to see if he was the man he pretended to be. He must have had a vision of what a jet-setting millionaire was supposed to do on his yacht, and he was playing that role. She was a happy-go-lucky forty-something who wore tight clothes, even though she weighed three hundred pounds, and spent hours getting ready each morning trying to look ten years younger. Put the two of them together on a yacht, add a little alcohol, and *voila!* Who wouldn't take advantage of that?

The following day everyone seemed back to normal, and the cruise continued in Rockstar fashion. We danced on tables at night, watched sports on the big plasma TV during the day, and drowned our hangovers in whatever morning vegetable drinks we could muster up. We even took time to discuss work and make decisions about important issues. I suppose this made us all feel like normal employees who weren't floating around the ocean on some yacht, drinking and eating as if we had just hit the lottery.

I was getting paid a pretty penny to vacation and party my butt off. It would have been politically incorrect not to be a Rockstar. I think if any of us had been more focused on what we should have been doing, we would have appeared odd. I believe—and it's only my opinion—that my boss treated us so well in order to keep us at arm's length. My God, who would want to be the person to throw the wrench in such a great deal? The best way to win friends and influence people, I'm sure he reasoned, was to keep us well entertained and living life, if not in the lap of luxury, at least close enough nearby to want to remain right where we were.

I wish I could say that I had seen through him before he was caught absconding with company funds, but I hadn't. I always liked him and respected him as a businessperson. He was someone I looked up to and aspired to be like. He worked hard and played hard and seemed to care a great deal about his employees.

Unfortunately for him, the days of structured audits came to an end and someone he had hired himself blew the whistle on some suspicious accounting practices that pointed directly at him.

I am surprised, as you may be, that I didn't recognize the tools of the liar. If I had taken a step back and analyzed the situation, I would have seen that something didn't jibe. Why was he spending money as if there were no tomorrow when he was a CPA? That made no sense at all. But we were all too busy with our own lives to stop to think about it. I was no different than everyone else and was equally fooled by his kindness.

The day I learned what he'd been doing, I was sitting in my office when my assistant buzzed me to tell me that the captain of the yacht was on the telephone asking for me. I remember thinking, *Why me?* I didn't know the man from Adam. When I took his call, he told me I was the only person from our company whose last name he remembered. He asked me if my boss was in trouble with the IRS, because someone had come and confiscated his entire fleet of cars and the yacht. He said he was fired for no reason, along with the rest of the service staff.

I didn't know what was going on, but it sounded like it was pretty bad. I hung up and called my counterpart in another office. She was aware that something was wrong but was also unsure as to what.

That evening I had a meeting with my Leadership Class. The board of directors was supposed to be there with us, so I figured that would be my chance to find out what was going on. Once everyone arrived, I realized my boss wasn't there, and that confirmed my worries that something terrible had happened. I asked the COO if he had seen my boss, and he almost spilled his drink. He said simply, "He couldn't make it." I saw the truth in his eyes. Whatever was going on was obviously not going to be announced that night.

The news began to spread the next day. Rumors varied on the amount of money and the people involved, but the common thread was that my boss had embezzled millions. There were those who couldn't believe it and tried to rally in his favor, and there were those who were so dismayed that they cried. I fell somewhere in between. I wasn't shocked that someone would embezzle money—it was in the news all the time—but I was amazed that *he* was involved. It makes sense now, looking back at all the money he threw around, but he was someone I *admired.* The feeling of being fooled, of being completely oblivious to what was going on, caught me off guard. I had prided myself on reading people and chose the people I looked up to very carefully.

For the rest of the day, I couldn't stop thinking about sitting on the yacht—the one purchased with all that stolen money—drinking wine and eating food with this person and thinking what a great guy he was. I had never wondered why he was so reckless with money, spending like there was no tomorrow. I know now that it was because he realized there may not be.

His lies must have haunted him even during those good times, just as mine did. The yacht probably never felt real. He probably never felt as if it belonged to him or that he had earned it on his own, and therefore who cared if we danced on the tables or spilled wine on the floor?

His lie was a whopper compared to mine and, in no uncertain terms, *definitely* a crime. But I feel I had a different perspective on it than most people because of my own situation. I actually felt sorry for him. I wanted to know how everything with him had started fifteen years earlier. Whether out of morbid curiosity or a fanatic desire to compare his situation to mine, I wanted to know more. Was he desperate for money for some noble cause and everything thereafter simply spiraled out of control? Did he have a gambling habit? Was he simply consumed by the idea of being wealthy?

He had a wife, teenage children, and friends and colleagues who knew him as a good man. He had an identity beyond being rich. He was generous and driven and always willing to fight the good fight. He cared about the environment and his employees' well-being. He had a personality and an image and a place at the company. People *knew* him.

Besides all the money, he lost everything that day. He lost everything he had become, and no one was going to remember anything positive about him. He had lived every day of the past fifteen years as someone he was not. For that, I felt bad for him. Even worse, he was probably going to face finding his true self during long hours spent behind bars.

I wonder if he ever wanted to stop but just couldn't. I also wonder if I am giving him too much credit. Maybe he loved scamming everyone, and maybe he took us on the yacht just so he could laugh about it later. Maybe he went home afterward and snickered to himself about how blind we all were.

I don't think so, because if he had been embezzling for fifteen years, he began doing it in his twenties. Was he, like me, a victim of the inability to think beyond some sugarcoated version of what his life should be? I'm betting he thought he was smarter than everyone else and deserved what he was taking. I'm betting somewhere in there was the good guy we all saw on the outside, except poorer. He will live forever with a mistake he started in his twenties—and he will live part of that mistake in prison.

Sure, he could have stopped it after the first million. Or the third. But at what cost? Would it have been worth all he has lost, or would it have been better to have gained less then? Would he be less of a criminal if he'd embezzled only $20 million . . . or $10 million . . . or $5 million?

I'm certain he had days where he thought of turning himself in but couldn't do it. The cost to himself and his family would be too great. There must have been days when he felt trapped and unable to enjoy even the simpler things in life. I wonder if he struggled through his thirties without being able to find himself, and I wonder what he felt looking in the mirror every day at someone who had all the respect and admiration he ever wanted—but knew it wasn't really his.

He had taken a wrong turn somewhere and ended up living the life of someone else. Now that life was going to be taken away. I wonder if he was able to enjoy even one brief moment of relief. I wonder who stood by him and who didn't.

Even seeing the differences between what I was doing and what he had done, I could draw all too easily on the similarities of how we both likely felt and what we both lived through. I don't think he was a heartless, guiltless criminal, although I realize those people do exist. I don't think that because I knew the upstanding person he was trying to be.

He was obviously extremely intelligent and raised two decent children. I wondered if any of his early success had stemmed from over-compensating to cover up for his perceived shortcomings. Other than embezzling the money, he appeared on the outside to live a very moral life. Even the episode on the boat wasn't that big of a deal. I don't know whether his wife knew about the embezzlement, but I would have to believe his kids didn't. I can't imagine having to come clean to your nearly grown children about something like that.

Yet here I was with my own daughter approaching her preteen years, thinking all the while that her mommy had graduated from college. I couldn't help but wonder what effect it would have on her if I were to go through a similar situation. I wouldn't be able to defend myself by telling her there are worse liars out there than I. That wouldn't make any sense to her, especially at her age. I was her mommy, and I wasn't supposed to lie or try to be someone I am not. These are the fundamental values kids are expected to follow, and they instinctively expect them from grown-ups, especially their own parents. My manufactured image was that of someone to be respected and admired, but my real self was some weakling hiding behind my excuses for not wanting to take back my life.

My marriage was also at stake. It seemed too late in the game to come clean now. If he had begun to dislike me already, my confessing would have provided my husband with the perfect excuse to leave me. Everyone would understand his reasons. It would be a deal breaker, and I wasn't ready to fail at marriage for the second time. I didn't feel forgiveness would even be an option for him. He could walk out the door vindicated, secure in the knowledge that his new ex-wife was a loony-toon liar who faked everything and therefore deserved to be left alone. I had entered into the marriage as a phony and led him to believe I was something more than I was. Finding out the truth would be reason enough for him to move on.

Once again I felt alone and abandoned, to the point of despair. I had no one to bounce my thoughts off of, no one to cry to when I was scared. I was wading through the ever-deepening waters of my own deceit and couldn't manage to get my thoughts straight.

I knew I had three choices: I could keep quiet and keep plugging away; I could turn myself in—confess to one and all—and hope for the best; or I could get out of Dodge before I got caught.

Even after seeing the destruction caused by my boss, I wasn't ready to give up my imaginary life, so leaving town was out of the question. I didn't know what repercussions I might face if I turned myself in, and I was pretty sure I didn't want to find out. That left choice number one.

I decided the best way to get on with my life was to strengthen the walls that I had built around myself so long ago. If I did that, I could put aside my mounting paranoia and get back to living the life I knew. An investigation was already under way and I realized that everyone in the accounting department would be coming under scrutiny. My turn would come, and I would be unflappable. After all, my lie paled in comparison, and they were looking for bigger fish than I to fry.

During those early days of the investigation, my fellow Rockstars were stunned, especially the one I knew had been exchanging tongues with the boss only months earlier. She wrote an e-mail to the group saying she couldn't believe what had happened and how much she *loved* him. She meant it in a friendly way, but I understand she came under fire for that e-mail later on.

She was cleared in the investigation, but the fact that they had held her under a microscope meant that everyone was being watched, every move recorded. I couldn't blame them, of course. The amount of money that was missing was astonishing, and the investigators must have realized that others had to be involved.

Before long, several other people were fingered for their participation—none of whom surprised me much.

Only recently, I heard that my boss had been sentenced to serve ten years in prison. The other people involved each received five years or so. I think of them from time to time in their cells and try to imagine how horrible it must be. I think it would probably be worse to go to prison after having been rich than having been poor. For my boss, time behind bars would be in stark contrast to days spent sailing the world on the yacht and dining in five-star restaurants.

Ten years is a long time.

# CHAPTER NINETEEN

A new set of nightmares began shortly after my boss was charged with embezzlement. They made my old panic attacks look like a walk in the park. The attacks had been devastating, but they were relatively easy to forget once they were over. The nightmares caused me to lose sleep and stayed with me for days after I had them.

The nightmare was always the same. I was in prison and my family forgot about me. I was calling everyone I knew on the phone, and no one would answer. I sat in my cell waiting to make my one phone call and then dialed the numbers—in slow motion—and no one would ever answer. I was in a lonely, cast-out hell and no one cared.

I imagined my daughter living life without me and wondering why even *she* wouldn't pick up the phone. I felt I deserved better than that, and I remember having a tangible feeling of regret every time I woke up. The nightmare made me sick to my stomach, but I was helpless to stop it. Even though I knew prison was not in my future, I couldn't shake the fear or the bad feelings that came out at night. In the wee hours of morning, after waking up sweating and crying, it seemed possible that someone was trying to tell me something. But who? During the day I could write the dreams off as stress disorder or sleep deprivation, but during those nights I couldn't. I would have done anything to stop the dreams from coming. They were wearing me down and making me worry about what was yet to come.

I expressed my fears to my husband, and we had some heart-to-heart talks about the situation at work. I wanted to feel him out about my future—to find out what he thought I should do—and could have smacked him for how simplistic his responses were. He said whatever I wanted to do was fine; he would support me either way. Sometimes I yelled at him and put him down because he wasn't giving me any real advice—something I could use, something I could rely upon, an easy way out. The demons surrounding my future seemed like everything to me and nothing to him. I felt as if he didn't understand the severity of what I was talking about. He acted as if my job could come and go and no one would really care. I couldn't get the response I felt I needed, and that just fed my anxiety. Of course, he couldn't possibly understand what I was talking about because he was still blissfully clueless to the underlying problem creating all the bubbles. He viewed me as someone strong and untouchable because that is who I had led him to believe I was.

He thought if I left my job I could get an even better one. He had no idea I would be pulling the rug out from under our lives and had the power to destroy us while at the same time lacking the power to get it back.

Was this only one more example of me looking in the mirror and not seeing things how they really were, or was I becoming mentally unstable and making mountains out of molehills? My mind was screaming out the questions, but I was getting no responses. The nightmares kept coming every evening, and the sun kept rising every morning.

I felt very alone in the following days and I know that I created the void all on my own. I felt as if I had made so many mistakes that I was trapped inside my own life—I had locked myself up in my beautiful prison and somehow misplaced the key. I couldn't talk about my situation with anyone. I am certain it was difficult to hear me complain. Poor little successful rich girl. Poor little me. I mean, what did I think it would be like to have a career such as mine, making all that money?

A walk in the park? I am sure my husband thought I sounded ridiculous, especially since I had always made myself appear so tough and independent and impenetrable.

I claimed never to cry, and I rarely did. When I did, I was almost always alone. Someone told me once that pain is weakness leaving the body. The implication is that once all the pain stops, we are stronger. Or are we just unable to feel pain because we have stopped feeling altogether?

I had forged an image of stoicism: the Ice Princess. That had served me well professionally. But now I had to deal with feelings that existed outside of the machine. Unfortunately, no one knew that, by my own design.

I suffered through my guilt and regret all alone, and rationalized that it was all my own fault. I had isolated myself and expected people to see me a certain way. If I said or did anything outside of what was expected, what would people think? Everything I had buried for so long just kept bubbling higher and higher. But I had to keep it at bay; I had to keep it inside. I was a cog, and I had chosen to be a cog.

My ride on the whirly-whirl was becoming insufferable. Little did I know, the worst was yet to come.

# CHAPTER TWENTY

Following the fall of my boss and the discovery of his embezzlement, everyone at the office was on high alert. Rumor had it that additional background screening for all employees would be coming down the pike soon, and this had become the number one topic around the water cooler. Everyone was going to be examined under the microscope—and that included me.

I thought about resigning. I wanted to resign. But I feared that would only trigger more scrutiny. People would think that I had something to do with my boss's handiwork. I was, after all, still a high-powered, well-paid manager. My leaving so suddenly would seem odd at best.

And as much as I hated my job, I still cared about what people thought of me. I didn't want them to think I had been involved in my boss's debacle, but if I left before the smoke cleared I knew the rumors would start flying. The rumor mill was already out of control, and I didn't want to be its next victim. In fact, I probably would have stuck it out through that entire period had the banished one not suddenly reappeared on the scene. I never saw it coming.

She worked for the man who was temporarily assigned to fill the seat of my former boss. He was an old, old, old-timer and it made sense for him to step up to try to stabilize the firm while all the pieces were falling where they would. He brought with him a reputation for damage control at its finest, with an impeccable reputation for being a hardcore pain in the ass. The banished one was his right-hand gal and was swept in right along with him.

It didn't help matters any that my former boss had been on the train that had derailed her years earlier. She relished being back in the action, and I could sense she was going to do whatever it took to destroy the careers of those she perceived had crossed her in the past. I had to be somewhere near the top of the list. I imagined her sitting in the dark in her living room, laughing like the devil incarnate. I imagined her relishing every agonizing moment.

Our accounting group had daily phone updates and meetings, and she was part of everything again. Her boss—suddenly my new boss— treated me like a kindergartener, most likely because of her feedback on me, and this just fueled my misery. She sounded happier than I had ever heard her sound, and that made a lot of people nervous.

One fateful day, the Rockstars, my new boss, the banished one, several board members, and I were all on a conference call with the accounting group. We were talking about the new committees being formed to investigate the embezzlement, and I volunteered to man one of them. Out of the blue I heard my new boss ask me if I understood the chain of command. I politely told him I didn't understand the question. He then repeated loud and clear, "Do you understand the chain of command?"

I was shocked and angry—angry as hell. I sat there stunned for several seconds before pulling the receiver back from my ear and staring at it. The keypad stared back silently. I racked my brain for a response. Here I was, trying to help, and he had attacked me for it. Was he upset because I had offered my time without checking with him first? I only had a moment to think it through, and I couldn't think of any other explanation for his comment. Fury flickered inside me. I wasn't used to being treated that way. It was the final straw. Even though no one could see it, I flicked my phone the bird and slammed it down onto the cradle. I was not going to be belittled in front of my peers by this man.

For the first time in years, I felt free. For the first time in my life, I felt like me.

Later that same day I sent my resignation to him via e-mail. Before long, members of the board of directors began to call me and beg me to stay. They told me he was only temporary and I wouldn't have to deal with him anymore. I no longer cared. I was high on being me. I was sailing on my boat, leaks and all. I didn't need anyone else's approval or permission. I was finally sick of being a phony.

The internal war between my fake persona and the real me had come to a head. Luckily, against the odds, the real me had sustained some power over the years and had made a comeback. The real me didn't have a plan, but the beautiful thing was that the real me didn't care. All I wanted to do was go home and hug my daughter. I couldn't wait to tell her I quit my job. The best part was that I knew she would be happy. She would be happy for me and thrilled for herself.

I went home and told my family the news. They were surprised, but not shocked. The first thing they wanted to know was what I was going to do next. I suppose, since I had just cut the family income by nearly six figures a year, that was a fair enough question.

But, frankly, I didn't know. I didn't want to do anything. All I wanted to do was pick my daughter up from school each day. But I couldn't get a paycheck for that. Not good. My husband was very understanding on the surface, but I know people well enough to realize that he was squirming on the inside. I had pulled the rug out from under us, and it appeared as if I had done so because of a single ridiculous telephone call.

I tried to explain that there was more to it than that, and he said he was fine with whatever I wanted to do, but I saw what I saw. I saw him squirm. That scared me. I wondered to myself if I wasn't finally just going crazy. I wondered if I had just made the biggest mistake of my life. I had just walked out on thousands of dollars a month. I had just left behind an income I couldn't possibly re-create without compromising the very principles I had left it for. Was I merely being a spoiled brat who was incapable of criticism? Were my feelings of relief unfounded? Had I accidentally traded in the lesser of the two evils?

But even in the cloud of doubt and fear I felt relief: true, undeniable relief. I felt real and clean, as if no one could hurt me now. I had yanked the rug out from underneath myself, but at least I hadn't let anyone else do it. I felt I had walked through the forest and, while afraid at times, had managed to escape with my life. That was it. I was alive. I was still alive. And free.

I spoke with some people at the firm, and, as expected, the rumors were flying about why I had left. Speculation was that I must have known what was going on with the embezzlement. I was surprised at how much that stung. I was surprised at how much I cared. I guess I was feeling righteous; I had just embarked on this path of honesty and somehow even that was being muddled by someone else's mistakes. I was mad at anyone who would think that about me. I wanted to call every one of them and tell them that not only would I never have done anything like what they were thinking but that I gave up all of my financial independence to do the right thing. And I did it on my own, without having to be called on the carpet. I did it because it was the right thing to do. I did it because I felt guilty for deceiving people I knew at work. I did it because it had *never* felt right. I did it because I grew up and became better than that. I did it because I was a good person. I was hurt by what they said, but the relief was stronger. I felt I had stepped back from the edge of the cliff and could finally take a look around without falling.

And then I realized that I needed a plan. We lived high on the hog, and one income just wasn't going to cut it. I tried to look at everything realistically and determined that I didn't need to make as much as I did before, but I did need to make some sort of decent money to keep our family's finances on track.

I didn't want to work as many hours, didn't want to travel, and didn't want anything to do with corporate America. Hmmmm. I sure did come up with some toughies. I could have sat down and brainstormed about what my dreams and aspirations were, but at the time I didn't realize that I had any. I hadn't totally grasped the concept that the real me was trying to escape a lifelong prison, and I didn't stop to consider what I really wanted from life. My emotions had been through so much turmoil, I felt as if I simply wanted to stand still—just grind to a halt and not make a move. Unfortunately, that is an impossibility in this world. The whirly-whirl keeps going around and forces us to move with it.

I wanted simplicity. I wanted a job that didn't control me. I didn't want to have to care about anything except family issues. I wanted something brainless, with no boss to worry about. I obviously needed to have my own business, but I knew that start-ups were a lot of work and frequently failed. I needed to buy an established business, something with good capital prospects. I had saved a nice nest egg in my retirement plan and could use that money to buy something if I had to.

I couldn't think—couldn't unwind long enough to think things through—so I decided to take a trip to the tanning salon.

I walked in and told the manager that I wanted the usual. We chatted a bit and I told her about quitting my job. She had the same question as everyone else: What was I going to do now? I told her that I honestly didn't know but that I might buy my own business if I could find the right opportunity. Her eyes lit up, and she told me the salon was for sale.

A tanning salon. I hadn't considered that before, and it didn't occur to me that a pale kid from the Midwest that the other kids used to call Snow could ever own a tanning salon. It was a pretty nice place and the lady who owned it seemed well off and happy. *Worth looking into*, I thought.

And look into it I did. The salon was already under contract to be sold, but I found another one and made an offer. However, my usually intuitive and brilliant decision-making skills were about to let me down. I bought the salon at a terrible time of year. Buying a tanning salon in the summertime in Florida is like buying an ice cream shop in New York in the middle of winter. It wasn't very smart, but it fit my requirements of being a no-brainer to run, sans corporate responsibilities, and all my own.

At first I enjoyed the quiet, but when the money wasn't what I expected, it became my new nightmare. I sat for hours without a customer, which was bad enough, but all that free time made me question the intelligence of leaving the big, fat paycheck that had made my family and me so happy. Not only did the salon not make me what I used to make, but after a couple months I wasn't even making a profit. It was actually costing me money to go to work. And I had hours upon hours to think about it.

I also began to realize that the tanning salon business failed to suit my personality. I didn't have any girlfriends in real life, and every woman who came in to the salon wanted to be best buds. Or worse. I had a regular customer who came in every other day and, without fail, asked me to rub her tanning lotion on her back. Worse yet, she always called for me when she was already in her room and half undressed. I don't think she meant it as a pass at me. I honestly think she was lonely and rich and just wanted to show off her expensive underwear. She was sometimes three sheets to the wind when she arrived and hardly able to stand as I applied the lotion to her back. I felt bad for her, but at times I felt even worse for myself.

I would go through our bills on the computer and run different scenarios to try to make the numbers fit. It was fruitless even to try. We were in trouble financially—serious trouble. Some days I couldn't breathe because it scared me so much.

My husband was clueless about our financial situation. Through the years I had always handled the bills and had never had any problem paying them with our dual income. Since wiping out half of our income, I was having difficulty making ends meet for the first time in years. I had been broke before, but this was a different kind of broke. This was the kind of broke where bill collectors started calling if I got behind on a payment. In fact, they started calling my husband at work. It had been only four months since I bailed on corporate America, and my ship was taking on water. I was going to sink.

We had a huge mortgage payment, hefty car payments, and numerous other payments—too many to mention. The numbers were not working, and I was terrified.

We began borrowing against our house, filling out credit card applications we received in the mail, and even borrowing against my husband's 401(k). I couldn't afford to pay employees at the salon, so I ended up working eighty hours a week myself. It was a nightmare. I felt I was being paid back for the lies I had told and had profited from for so long. In fact, I was *sure* of it. I was failing at my very first attempt to be myself.

In late 2005, when we couldn't come up with the money for our mortgage payment, I looked down at my $7,000 Rolex and decided it was time to start getting rid of the things I didn't deserve. I sold it for $3,000 and paid our mortgage with the money. I cried a lot that day—not about the watch, but about who I had been and who I had become. I felt like a loser, like I had let everyone down. My family was miserable, when I only wanted to make them happy. In fact, I had counted on them being happy. I was afraid that I had misjudged the real world. The ideals on which I had based my decision suddenly seemed as if they existed only in the movies. This was real life and we had real bills and real bill collectors. They didn't give a damn that I had done the *right* thing. Bills couldn't be paid with morals. No one cared what I had given up, or why.

As if that weren't bad enough, I soon realized that I was no longer the high-powered executive wearing expensive suits, and I no longer garnered respect from anyone. I no longer had anyone kissing up to me—and I honestly missed it. The girls I hired to work at the salon a few hours a week couldn't have cared less what I really thought about them. I wore shorts, a T-shirt, and flip-flops to work and lacked any sophistication whatsoever. No one who came in wanted to talk about stocks; they were there to relax and gossip about their hairdressers. I no longer walked in a room and felt important. I no longer felt in charge. It was a far cry from the status I had once commanded as a boss in corporate America.

Oddly, I had never realized that my identity had been tied so tightly to something so superficial, but it had. I had enjoyed people looking up to me, even if the me they looked up to wasn't real. The respect they showed and the envy I saw in their eyes was something to be missed, and miss it I did. I lost a part of me when I lost that. I think it is because I always tried to be a good leader for my group, and *that* part of me was legitimate. The respect and affection I felt from my employees was legitimate. There were times when I even missed the ridiculous meetings I had grown so tired of. I missed those moments when I could take the floor and feel all eyes on me. I missed those times when I knew I had said and done everything right with everyone watching. Those moments couldn't be discounted. But they also couldn't outweigh the high price I had paid to get them. I knew I had based much of my self-worth on those moments, and now those moments were over and my image was suffering.

If I wasn't the person who could take charge of a roomful of high-powered executives anymore, then who was I? Did I have talent enough to succeed at something else? If I walked into a room without a power suit on, would anyone even look up? I had become a certain charismatic character in a costume. Without the costume, the character no longer made sense. Was there enough of a person under that costume to make it in the world? Or had I simply come full circle back to the days when I was being myself—and failing?

Was I about to pull up to the restaurant in my piece-of-crap car, walk through the front door, and fall down right in front of my client? Had I taken the wrong road based on some superficial idea of what we as human beings are supposed to do with regard to right and wrong? Maybe these righteous morals had a place only in Sunday school. There, the kids could believe that dinosaurs never existed and that grown-ups don't lie. "Right and wrong" is black and white. Maybe I had tried to apply ridiculously simplistic ethics to real life, where they couldn't possibly hold water. Maybe we were supposed to grab life as it came and roll with whatever decisions we made, right or wrong. We get only one trip around the whirly-whirl, and if we take the short road and no one gets hurt, why should we derail ourselves?

I am not sure to this day whether it was dame fortune or bad luck, but either way the decision had already been made. I had traded in my fancy costume for an attempt to be myself. Things weren't looking good, it's true. But I was still filled with hope that things would get better. I know, looking back, that feeling hopeful during that time in my life was an indication that I would survive. I never gave up and I never stopped trying to solve the problem, whatever it might have been on any given day. Life does not have a rewind button, and any time spent wishing it did is simply wasted time. I had moments of doubt about what I had done—many moments—but I was always looking toward the future. I only hoped that that would be enough.

I tried to forge ahead and be strong, somehow managing to rob Peter to pay Paul. The salon required very little of my thoughts, merely my presence, and I had endless hours to devote to worry. I didn't have any money to spend on advertising or anything that would require planning, so I focused on how to fix things outside of the salon.

In my worst hours, I cried and held my dogs. Each of them had a unique personality and a unique response to my tears. The best part was that none of them judged me. None of them knew or cared whether I graduated from college or had a good job or dressed well. They treated me the same and were happy to see me no matter what. They sat still and quiet while I held them and let out my tears—tears I couldn't let out in front of anyone else because they would be terrified.

But my dogs were not terrified; they were happy to be touched and paid attention to. They were soft and furry, and it was like having real, live teddy bears to drown my sorrows in. They didn't care that they had to eat a different kind of food when we couldn't afford the better brand. They never cared what kind of watch I wore. I never saw an inkling of doubt flash in any of their eyes. They remained true and loyal and sweet through my toughest days. They remained happy—in fact, happier, because I saw them more. I even took them to the salon when I could. Those days with my dogs made the pain less painful somehow. Dogs have a way of living in the moment that I could only envy during that period in my life. No worries about who was calling or what was due. They were a bright spot for me, something I could hang on to that was a consistently positive note in my life. They were there for me without ever knowing it, and I am grateful to this day.

The hole I was in was getting deeper every day and the hopelessness was becoming unbearable. I had caused my family extreme financial hardship. For what? To cleanse my own guilty conscience? To make matters worse, I had tried to take on this new venture and was failing for the second time in my life. I certainly wasn't getting a warm fuzzy feeling from the powers that be about having made a good choice. I couldn't take back what I had done, but I couldn't keep going down this same path. I put the salon up for sale and decided I needed to take charge of my life.

I sat down and decided to map out my Happy Pie again. This time the pie was much different. My career piece was very small, my money piece frighteningly small, and my family piece huge. Putting it in the context of the Happy Pie explained why it wasn't working. Putting 100 percent of my passion into my family wasn't the answer. It wasn't enough to make me a whole person. I needed a career I cared about, I needed to be able to pay my bills, and I needed to spend quality time with my family.

It was a real "Duh" situation, but until I put it in the chart I didn't realize it. I think I had missed my family for so long that I put too much focus on that and in turn lost the other two things that drive me. I realized that life is a balance of myself and those around me. My family loved me and wanted me around, but they loved to see me succeed and also loved some of the finer things in life. It was okay to love those things. It was okay to love working. It was okay to be passionate about my job. I saw that my lack of satisfaction in corporate America stemmed from my own dishonesty, not from some internal laziness or evilness of the corporate machine. If I hadn't lied to get where I got, I may have ended up happy there. I will never know, but I suppose that is for the best.

During my stay in corporate America, I had developed skills to go with my drive, and I learned what it took to be successful. I just had to find something new, a different opportunity in which to put them all to work. I owed it to myself to get my pie balanced once and for all.

Even with the salon a complete disaster, I figured I had gotten it partially correct. I needed something that was flexible and that I could do on my own without any real supervision. That left out corporate America. I had to find something for the real me that I was passionate about. I had purchased the salon because I wanted to focus on my family and didn't want to put my heart into my work, but that was the wrong perspective. I needed to find a career that I was passionate about while still remaining true to myself and my family. I asked myself what my one true passion in life has always been, and the answer was obvious: animals. I had always enjoyed bringing my dogs to the salon with me and thought some sort of pet-sitting or doggie daycare center might be right up my alley.

The salon sold fairly quickly, because the tanning season was approaching. I focused all my efforts on a business plan for a doggie daycare. I calculated what a facility would cost and the possible profits. I visited several in the area and talked to whoever would answer my questions. I felt ten years younger and felt more motivated than I had in a decade. The simplest tasks related to the venture were thrilling. I determined that I needed to know more about dogs than just how cute they were if I wanted to go into business babysitting them. Watching people's dogs was similar in nature to watching people's children: such a business would carry a lot of responsibility. But that didn't bother me. I wanted to do this right and have an edge on my competitors, so I decided to get certified as a dog trainer through an accredited school.

I found a school with an excellent reputation, and, just as important, a school loan program so that I didn't have to pay until I got a job. I finished the six-month course in a matter of weeks and prepared to do my internship. I had to do twelve hours under an established trainer, and the school helped me locate someone in my area. Together, we set out to complete my certification.

I worked hands-on helping train dogs in basic obedience, and I loved every second of it. I had so much fun that I found myself bouncing out of bed each day. I dressed quickly and sped off to the kennel. My trainer was impressed by my enthusiasm, and we talked about the possibility of my working for her. I was thrilled and flattered by the offer, and the position seemed to have a lot of potential. I gave up my plan for my own facility and jumped on board. I wouldn't be making very much money at first, but even that was better than the running deficit I had experienced at the salon. My career piece had just gotten bigger, without sacrificing any of my family piece, and even my money piece was looking up. I was off to a good start.

I called my dad to tell him everything that was going on. He was happy to hear that I had shed myself of the salon. When I told him about my new job and how excited I was, he suggested I draw pictures of each dog that I trained and try to sell them to the owners. I told him I couldn't really overstep the boundaries of what I was hired to do, since it wasn't my business and that might upset my boss. He told me to draw a picture of her dog for her and see what she thought. It seemed silly at the time, but I thought I'd humor Dad. Besides, I wanted to show my boss my appreciation for taking me on, so I grabbed a picture of her dog off her Web site and went to work.

Although it had been years since I'd done any serious drawing, I was glad to see that my skills hadn't abandoned me. If anything, I seemed to have gotten better somehow. Best of all, I felt good doing the picture and couldn't wait to show it to my boss.

She raved over the picture and insisted I do some others for our clients—clients willing to pay for them, of course. She became my biggest fan and spread the word about my artwork to everyone she met. At times I felt uncomfortable selling my art, which had always been so personal to me. It seemed almost unfair to charge money for something that doesn't cost me anything but time to make, but it was empowering and flattering that these people would entrust me to create something they hung up in their homes. The best part was that I was doing pictures of their pets—dogs, cats, birds, and horses. I enjoyed bringing the portraits to life using detail in the eyes and the personalities in their facial expressions. I charged a couple hundred dollars for each and was thrilled to get that for my work.

My dad was elated for me—possibly for the first time in my life. He wanted to talk about what I was drawing and who was buying my work and how to make my portraits even better. I heard the excitement in his voice, and I heard something else, as well: pride. He was finally proud of me.

He didn't care how much I was getting paid; he knew I was doing something that made me happy. He was sixty years old and breathing a sigh of relief. His advice had not gone unheeded. The irony did not escape me. The first thing I had ever done to earn his pride was drawing. Now, once again, after finally finding the real me, my artistic talents were once again drawing his praise. The whirly-whirl has a way of coming full circle, remember? My father's approval meant more to me that day than at any other time in my life.

It made me stop and wonder what kind of lessons I was teaching my own daughter. Had I gotten lazy and overlooked a lie here and there and forever altered her ability to determine right from wrong? How much of an effect did I have on my baby girl just by being too kind to call her out on not brushing her teeth when she swore she did but I knew otherwise? Maybe it will cost her only a cavity—but maybe it will cost her more. Maybe it will hone her acting skills and tempt her into taking the short road one too many times. Did all those years watching me parade around in my heels and perfume make her want to emulate me at any cost? She was only eight, but certainly that was an age at which I could have made an impression.

Whatever I had done to influence her, I realize, might take decades to come to fruition. I could only start in the present to make sure her path is something she chooses wisely and honestly. Today, she wants to be an obstetrician. Or maybe she thinks I want her to be an obstetrician, so she tells me that because it's what I want to hear. There's no way of knowing for sure.

What I do know is that she has a passion for babies and watches all those baby delivery shows the way other kids watch SpongeBob. She seems passionate about birthing and obstetrics, and I've entered her room on numerous occasions to find eight or nine sick baby dolls in all areas of the room with all kinds of life-support systems (straws, wire) taped to them with Scotch Tape. Maybe she is lucky to know what her passion for life is so early on. I will certainly make it clear to her how much education she'll need to be an obstetrician and I will encourage her to get it—honestly.

I also fear what my daughter will think of this book. She is now ten and very keen and mature for her age. I have decided not to hide it from her. I am done hiding and covering up, even if there is good reason to do so. I hope she can take a positive lesson from my mistakes and slow down her own personal whirly-whirl. I want her to think about her decisions in life and make them based on truth and happiness. I know she will make mistakes, and that is fine—everybody does—but I hope they turn out to be minor ones that don't trap her in a false world from which she feels she cannot escape. As soon as she is old enough, I am going to help her construct her own Happy Pie. Her pieces will be different when she is younger and change as she ages, and I'll tell her that is fine. If she wants my help, even after the debacle

I created, I'll be there to give it to her. I want her to see that it's okay to try and fail, and it's okay to want things that she doesn't see everyone else wanting. I will teach her that it's okay to like money and respect and it's also okay if she doesn't care about those things at all. I will help her keep her real self on the surface at all times and stand up for herself when faced with anything that challenges who she really is.

She is smart enough to find the short road on her own, but I imagine I will be beside her telling her always to check out the long road too. She doesn't go to Sunday school, and she has questions about things that remind me so much of myself at that age. She is going to struggle with her own self-awareness, but she is more confident than I was, and I think she will handle herself well. She is an excellent student, and I will encourage her to get a college education *if* that's in keeping with her goals. I will stand back and let her make her mistakes, and my heart will bleed for her. I only hope she can understand all the things I did and how important she was to me throughout all of it.

Most of all, I hope she grows up slowly. She is ten and already has a cell phone and social events to attend. She is five feet tall and appears to be about fourteen. I hope she is not cursed with my drive to be a grown-up as quickly as possible. The world is there for the taking, and I hope she takes it little by little, one piece at a time. I want to tell her that I'm sorry for all that I missed and that I intend to keep her as my focus until she no longer needs me to.

I will also stress the importance of being a whole person and having a balanced Happy Pie. The pieces of her pie may differ from mine, but they will need to be balanced nonetheless. Just being a doctor won't make her happy. But not being a doctor could very well make her unhappy. There is more to the whole picture than only one piece of pie. I hope I am able to explain that to her in a way that makes an impact. I wish it had been explained to me earlier in my life. In a way, I guess it was: My father wanted me to be happy and my mother wanted me to be successful—both merely pieces of my greater Happy Pie.

# CHAPTER TWENTY-ONE

*Hero worship.* What a wonderfully complex, delightfully rich, ridiculously phony concept businesspeople all around the world cling to. We worship the legends in our industry. We worship the corporate big shots. We worship our immediate supervisors. Did you ever stop to wonder why we rarely worship anyone lower on the corporate ladder than we?

Yet hero worship is based in fantasy. Now, years after I indulged in the concept and bowed beneath the lights, I have the benefit of being able to step out of that role and into the life of a nobody. I saw my relationship with others fall by the wayside overnight. I witnessed people around me go from ON to OFF the moment I resigned. I practically got whiplash by how quickly I turned into a nobody, a nonentity, a never-was.

But that never stopped me from craving the spotlight. At least not until I could no longer accept all those accolades for being someone I really wasn't. I felt I didn't deserve the fake ON feedback I got from most people. I was only ON to them because they thought I was influential. In time, I could no longer deal with that, and my intolerance grew exponentially out of my control.

Why couldn't I be happy having people love me on the surface? Life would have been so much easier if I had continued to laugh all the way to the bank and kept my conscience under control. Why did my mind begin to turn on me after I got everything I wanted? My life in the shallows began to wane and my priorities began shifting right before my eyes. Things I thought I had figured out and taken care of became skewed. What exists in the human soul to make us want to do the right thing? I don't know the answers to that question, but in my life, it was undeniable.

I have no doubt that college is a necessary tool for many professions. I certainly wouldn't want some doctor who only graduated from high school removing a brain tumor from my skull, but certainly there are instances where a degree is less than necessary. Is it true that the only way we can differentiate the more valuable businesspeople from the masses is to make their possession of a sheepskin the deciding factor?

I had success early on in life doing something I thought I wanted to do. I paid the price in many ways. I lost ten years of my life pretending to be someone I was not. My family and I suffered financially, emotionally, and mentally while I was trying to rid my life of the lies.

Part of the price I paid for maintaining my facade is that I never made any real friends as an adult, and now I miss friendship. The person I was trying to be was two-dimensional. There was nothing on which to base any true friendships. I could never reveal the real me, so I never forged any friendships that could last. People I socialized with wanted to use me either to get ahead or for their sexual gratification. That's what the corporate world seemed to consist of. I was part of the club of powerful people, and we made each other more powerful by hanging around in groups. I don't talk to anyone I used to work with. Once I became a nothing, I no longer mattered to them—and I can't say that they were exactly high on my list of priorities. I couldn't offer anyone career advancement or a raise. I couldn't sit at their meetings and nod my approval. They couldn't give me their undying devotion.

There was a time a couple years ago when all my lunch hours were booked weeks in advance with people who just wanted a piece of my time. I haven't had lunch with a friend for as long as I can remember. I haven't gotten to gossip or dish or do any of the things that real friends do.

It hurts to know that everyone I knew back then was a manifestation of my own lack of self-esteem. It was hero worship. Those people who pretended to like me were only using me. Or perhaps if they did like me, they didn't like me enough to maintain a friendship once I fell off the corporate radar. Either way, I suffer to this day for not having any friends. It is my own fault for keeping everyone at a distance and lying about who I was. Some people along the way tried to penetrate my armor, but most were unsuccessful. If anyone got too close, I simply shut him out of my life. If I thought someone was a threat to my phony persona, I wouldn't return her telephone calls or back her up in meetings.

I must have seemed pretty shallow. I hope in some way I helped some people, and I regret that I couldn't take the opportunity to get to know them better, to be a true friend. I've gone without a friend now for more than a decade, and it's sad. I watch TV shows where groups of ladies have nothing in life but each other and manage to scrape through every major issue in their lives relying on their lasting bonds of friendship. I long for that feeling and hope that I can find it someday. I think I know how to be a good friend. Now that I don't have to hide my past anymore, I may find myself able to open up and let that third dimension begin to take shape. I look forward to that very much.

For those people in my life who feel lied to, let me apologize. I hope you can understand how I made such a huge mistake. I hope you can look past the dishonesty and see that most of what you saw was a real person. Most of what you saw was me just trying to keep up with my phony image. I met so many people I admired over the years, and I would hate to think they are bitter or disappointed. If I considered you a mentor, it was sincere. I admired people I wanted to be like in all ways.

Sure, there were times when I forged relationships to help disguise in my mind what was happening behind the scenes, but I usually met someone I legitimately liked in the process.

To my husband, I hope whatever I really am is okay. I hope your disappointment in me can be overcome, and I hope that trust is something we can continue to work on. I don't deserve for anyone to stand by while I sink, but I am grateful for the depths of your understanding. The water under the bridge runs dark and deep.

And my poor parents. I love them endlessly. I am sure this is not what they had hoped I would become: a phony and a fake. How proud they will be. I suppose I should skip the next few family reunions until the smoke clears. I hope they understand my need to be objective and honest at this stage in my life. I need to start fresh. To all the other people in my life, please don't feel foolish or as if you were buffaloed. I made fooling people my number one goal in life—an art form—not because I wanted to but because I felt I had to. Ten years of being a phony honed my skills well, and everything that could have clued you in to my real identity was well hidden and mostly out of reach. Maybe some of you feel as if you knew something was amiss. If so, you may want to change careers and put your talents to better use working as an investigative journalist or an undercover cop for the local police department.

For those to whom I gave educational advice, I hope my being a hypocrite is not disenchanting. I hope you realize that my advice came from a place where I knew you would be better off. I knew what it was like to be you and to wonder where I was going and how I was going to get there. I hope I helped keep you from making missteps at an important time in your life. And I hope the school you returned to fit into your dreams and helped you find what you wanted most from life.

To those very few people who knew my secret, please understand that you are very special to me; you must have been for me to let you in. Thank you for supporting me and not asking too many questions. Thanks for acting like it wasn't a big deal during the times when it was all I could focus on. Thanks for seeing that there was a human being underneath all of that facade. Thank you for understanding that I can no longer trap myself in this image of something I will never really be.

My current career is so perfect for me and makes me so happy that I honestly wonder how I could have missed it from the start. I train dogs. I get to work with dogs every day and change people's lives as I teach their pets to become happy, well-adjusted members of their families. I have a flexible schedule and I work for a great company. My boss has run the same business for years. My life is much simpler now and makes so much more sense. My Happy Pie is finally balanced, and I can feel the results in my life.

Sure, I have hectic days and sometimes things don't go right, but I am able to deal with these things with a healthy mind and spirit and get over them much more quickly and easily than ever before. I no longer have the constant buzz of worry inside of me, driving everything I do. I don't have to pretend to be constantly ON. If I am smiling, I am really smiling.

I don't make the kind of money I used to make, of course, but we have worked hard to get our lifestyle within our new means and have recently had some success at that too. My family has sacrificed a great deal, but after a couple years of riding it out, we are starting to pull the financial purse strings together.

My job is important to me. My boss, who hates to be called that, is an extremely moral person. It is one of the things I admire about her. She is the type of person who will fight the right fight no matter what it costs her. She cares about people, animals, and the environment. She is a cancer survivor who I am certain has seen the dark days of fear and come to grips with who she is going to be for the rest of her life. Ethics, morals, and truth drive her character. She is a good person down to her very core, and, oddly enough, she believes in me. She trusts me implicitly, and I shudder at the thought that now she will know the terrible things I did.

I didn't lie on my current résumé. I didn't have to—no degree required to be a dog trainer. I got all the necessary certification by the book and have done things the right way so far. She knows I am only a high school graduate, but my problem is that I didn't tell her I lied about that at my previous job. She knows what I used to do for a living, and she is a smart person, so she may wonder how I had such a big job with no degree, but I didn't explain it. She has no idea about this huge revelation I am making. I don't know what she will think when she finds out, and that scares me. I don't want to lose what I have worked so hard to get. I have lost so much recently and this is something I really want to hold onto. I don't want to embarrass her or the company, but I cannot keep my past buried any longer. I will be devastated if she can't see past what I did or understand why I did it, but if that is a further price I must pay, then I will. I hope I don't embarrass too many people with this book, because that is certainly not my intent. I simply need to get this out in the open so that I can begin living life as the person I really am. I have had this monkey on my back for so many years that it is difficult to stop worrying about every little thing toppling you at any given moment.

I want to be someone who doesn't judge people based on their mistakes. I hope that all the people I know understand that they can come to me and confess anything they have ever done. I might be surprised, upset, hurt, or whatever, but I won't judge them. Life is full of opportunities to take the short road or the wrong road or the crazy road, and we are only human. Decisions we make one day can haunt us for years to come. I want to be a doorway for people to escape out of the traps they find themselves in unexpectedly. I, like you, didn't plan to let the lie get out of control. I didn't expect it to rule my life on a daily basis. I thought I could handle it, and I thought I could do the right thing when I could no longer justify the gains to myself.

But life is more complicated than that. People expect things of other people, and you come to expect things of yourself. We find things that give us pleasure, like possessions and respect, and we use those things to help bury our mistakes. We use those things to ease the anxiety created by our own lies.

Now, at long last, I needn't worry about someone tossing a monkey wrench and gumming up the works of my life. No one can harm me now—not even myself. Nothing can ever disrupt my new life as I know it again.

Except, perhaps, one little thing . . .

# CHAPTER TWENTY-TWO

*L*egal ramifications. I mentioned earlier that I never checked into what they may be. That's true to this day, and I hope I never have to find out. I worked hard for what I earned, and I did the best job I possibly could for the firms that hired me. I hope they can take some positive lessons from my exposé and put them to good use in the future.

There is no one watchdog for everything that happens in corporate America. Every human resources department is only as powerful as the authority its firm gives it. Privacy laws, First Amendment rights, and locked personnel files make checking up on employees difficult at best.

And yet everyone is not as he seems. You cannot be a good judge of character in all instances. Trust in your resources to have prospective employees checked out as thoroughly as possible. People who are trying to fool you will often seem more real than those who are not. Some have honed their skills to a degree you can't even imagine, and others, like myself, may not even know they're trying to fool you, which makes them the most dangerous people of all.

On the flip side, look beyond educational accomplishments for your leaders. Take the time to sift through the masses of people to find those who can rally your teams and lead them through times of crisis and adversity. Let go of your ego and trickle this message down to your managers. Get rid of the stereotype that a manager needs to be formally educated. A manager needs to have leadership skills and be willing to lead. Take a chance on people who are not the cookie-cutter version of yourself or your corporate officers. Give them a mentor and a support staff that can propel them and your firm into the future.

In my mind, while my moral compass may have been askew, I don't believe I ever acted illegally. I filled out all the paperwork and subjected myself to background checks. I worked hard for my employers and left when my heart was no longer in my job. During my various tenures, I turned departments around, led the charge to greater productivity and profitability, and helped find my successors upon my departure. I feel that I left each company for which I worked a little better, a little stronger, than it was when I began working for it.

Of course, I don't have all the answers, and I only have so many excuses. After all is said and done, I even have a few questions, such as why, after telling that first big lie, didn't I just keep going down the wrong road. Sure, I perpetuated the lie I told, but I didn't increase the level of wrongness of what I was doing. I didn't go from lying about a college degree to lying about my marital status or lying to others to get their jobs or embezzling funds. I never slept with anyone to get ahead. Something inside of me must have prevented me from taking the lie any further.

I know the difference between right and wrong. I know that what I did was wrong, but somehow I was able to justify it. When the well of justification ran dry, I stopped. I hope that means I'm a good person after all.

I never set out to trick people or get ahead just for the fun of ruining someone else's life. That was never my intention. I was a naive twenty-something who was too impatient to do anything I didn't want to do. I made a mistake and have learned so much from it. I gained a lot, but I lost a lot too. I lost time I can never get back. I lost some of myself I haven't found even yet. I harbor self-doubt and can't stop looking over my shoulder. I am faced with asking people to trust me when they really don't even know me. I can't find the rewind button, nor can I find the slow-motion switch. People will think what they want to about me no matter what I say, and if they decide never to speak to me again, I'll understand.

I hope the people I worked for consider themselves fortunate that I didn't head further down the path of self-destruction. Through no credit of my own, I drew a line in the sand and refused to cross it. Think of how many "phonies" there are out there who wouldn't hesitate to keep crossing that line until there was no more line to cross—like my former boss. Hiring a person like that could be disastrous, all because someone failed to be an adequate watchdog and screen prospective employees properly.

Of course, I doubt that any scrutiny of his résumé would have turned up anything suspicious on my former boss. But someone should have been watching the guy who handled all the money. That just makes sense. No matter how long he worked there or how great he seemed, someone should have been checking his work on a regular basis. If the opportunity for gain is great and the risk is small, many people will make the wrong choice. They may regret it later, but that usually doesn't matter at all. The damage gets done and the snowball continues down the mountain. Rarely does someone throw the wrench in themselves and call foul.

Which brings up something else I've been wondering. Just how many people *are* there who have lied their way through business? What percentage of our workforce is dishonest? How many have gotten where they are unethically?

Maybe we should hold a Get-Out-of-Your-Lie-Free Day—a national holiday for everyone who feels trapped behind their ill-created charades. A second chance for all good people to take a shot at just being themselves. An opportunity for companies to flush out some dishonesty without having to fire anyone and suffer the consequences of lost production. I know part of the risk of doing background checks retroactively is that the firm must act on what they have found. Throw that concept out the window for one day every year and make decisions based on what is best for the firm. Send a message to employees that they can be themselves and be forgiven.

You probably won't flush out the biggies—the embezzlers and such—but you might help enough of the little ones come out of the woodwork to set people's minds at ease so they can go on with their lives without fear of discovery and retribution.

In my case, a lack of maturity and a desperate need for money set me on the road to lying. In the end, what caused me to put an end to the charade was that I am a good person inside, and I was tired of lying. Good people are hard to find. Yet had I been outed at an earlier point in time, I'm certain I would have been terminated on the spot— and all the good I ended up doing for those people with whom I worked would have been lost.

Worse still from a personal point of view, I would never have found the opportunity to face my shortcomings and make the decision—as painful as it proved to be—to change. I would never have known the satisfaction of feeling that my integrity, for years clouded by necessity and greed, won out in the end. I would never have known the feeling of self-worth I know now.

Hopefully, it is not too little, too late.

# CHAPTER TWENTY-THREE

*eed and greed.* It is interesting how easily one can change into the other. Need can cause us to allow ourselves to act outside of what we believe is right. It's like the story of Robin Hood. He stole from the rich to give to the poor. He was stealing, but somehow that was okay because of why he was stealing and from whom. His reasons were justified. They were good enough. They made sense. In fact, they made him a hero.

We never stopped to think about the rich people and how hard they may have worked to get their money. We never questioned whether any of the poor people were lazy. It didn't matter, because Robin Hood was imaginary. He was just a two-dimensional image. But he taught us that sometimes even things that were wrong could be right if we had a good enough reason for doing them.

In my case, need turned to greed when I wasn't paying attention. I honestly feel I would not have gone down that road if I had not been so desperate to keep my daughter, but after I won that battle I couldn't stop myself. I made excuses, but the bottom line was that I got greedy—greedy not just for the money, but for the respect and self-worth I derived from being the boss. I justified my selfishness by spoiling my family with material things and ignoring my ever-increasing absence from their lives. I ignored or avoided anyone along the way who tried to point out anything I may have been doing wrong, and I shut out many potential friends who I'm sure will never understand why.

I tried to smother the dawning realization of my wrongdoing, but something inside kept building until I couldn't ignore it anymore. Just as with religion, I couldn't force myself to believe or appreciate any of the respect or love because I knew it wasn't real. I tried to help people along the way and was very generous in many situations. This did little to ease my ever-increasing self-doubt. No matter how many people I helped, it couldn't change the fact that I had traded my values for something I didn't deserve. No matter how many things I did right, I couldn't black out the number that I did wrong. I couldn't ever truly be the person I was pretending to be. I was a phony.

*The snowball effect.* What does it mean? It represents something that starts out small and simple but begins rolling downhill, out of control, all the while building on itself very quickly. It travels faster and faster, growing larger by the second, until it is a massive ball of snow and ice. Lies are a classic example of the snowball effect. It seems we can never tell only one simple lie and leave it at that. The fact is that lies do not fit neatly into the real world because they are not real. So when we try to piece them into reality, we discover that they shove other aspects of time and space out of whack. Then we need to tell another lie to explain the first. That leads to still more lies based on previous lies. Sometimes by the time we discover that the original lie is actually causing us harm, it is so large and going so fast that we can't imagine stepping out in front of it to stop it.

When life gets in the way of doing the right thing, the justification for perpetuating the lie seems logical and sane. We allow the lie to keep right on rolling and in turn sacrifice who we are, what we know is right, and our very reason for living in a desperate effort to stay out of our own way.

We long for the day when we can escape from underneath it and are terrified to think that day may never come. The snowball may never stop rolling—at least not until *we've* stopped rolling. It is so easy to live an entire lifetime, an entire trip around the whirly-whirl, as someone else—someone you felt you should have been, or had to be, or just wanted to be. It is so easy to misstep, take the wrong road, make the wrong choice. It's so difficult to remedy those decisions. If they are left to grow unchallenged, we suffer the consequences. We are damaged as people. We lack pride, identity, and depth.

If you are reading this book and have never lied, then by all means judge me. I deserve it. It would make sense to say that I suffered what I had coming to me, and the shift in lifestyle I experienced after quitting my job was a simple adjustment back to where I should have been to begin with.

That may be true, but I lost a lot more than lifestyle along the way. I lost my way. I lost my light. I nearly lost everything. In the end, however, I came away with a better understanding of who I really am and what is really important to me. I made some tough choices and gave up many things that I loved dearly and may never get to experience again. I have spent many nights lying awake wondering why I am doing what I'm doing. But I am committed to ending my life as a phony. I have decided I have to do this even though people are going to get hurt.

I spent the last decade of my life being someone I am not. I can never get that time back, but I can learn lessons from my loss and hope that part of that time was well spent. Maybe I simply needed to step back to see that I didn't like what I was pretending to be in order to appreciate who I really am. I missed opportunities for friendships and lifelong relationships based on my need for secrecy. I will never know how many wonderful things I blocked out during that ten-year period.

I will never know what would have been different or what personal growth and experiences I would have known had I never said that I had graduated from college. I cannot even begin to wonder whether I would have been better off. What I *can* say is that no matter how big the snowball becomes, there is always a way to stop it.

You may think that no one will understand or that your life would be reduced to shambles, but if you are struggling internally for something you are lying about every day of your life, you're paying too high a price. Giving in to the giant rolling snowball might make it look as though you've ruined your entire life. But the truth is that beneath all that snow, you can still find a solid foundation—enough, at least, to begin rebuilding a life based upon your real goals, the real you.

Lies are convenient when you tell them the first time, but they can become eternal nightmares that lead to your destruction. I uttered my first whopper *without stopping to think about it*, and it changed the course of my life for the next ten years. I thought I was smarter than everyone else, and it turns out I was mistaken. I am not smarter than everyone else, but I have a drive inside of me to be happy. I thought I could achieve that happiness by being what other people wanted or expected me to be, but life doesn't work that way. To be happy you have to determine your own pieces to the Happy Pie and take the shortcut only when it is appropriate. When it's not, take the long, arduous, more time-consuming route to get to your destination. It will pay dividends in the end. The long road may not be so much fun and will certainly not save you as much time, but it's an important part of life—and the time will pass no matter which way you choose.

As I write this, I am about to turn thirty-five, and the differences between what I deem important now and what I thought was important ten years ago are staggering. Back then I lacked any depth in my thinking and took one wrong turn after another. I am certain that time makes us wiser, so I may look back at this book ten years from now and wonder what I was thinking of when I started to write it.

I hope that doesn't happen. I hope I have gained some sort of maturity or sense or whatever it is that we gain with age, to make better decisions for myself. I have no idea what the future holds, nor do I focus on it as much as I used to. I spent so many years trying with all my might to get the whirly-whirl to spin faster, and now all I want it to do is slow down. The long road seems rather welcoming these days, rather embracing, as opposed to the daunting and perilous shortcut through life. And I still have a lot to learn.

I am not saying I will never take the short road again. I still believe in working smarter and not harder, but I won't compromise my ethics to do it and I won't let it take over the other parts of my life the way I did once . . . oh, so long ago.

I am willing to trade in my entire life up to this very moment for the person I now know I really am.

In the end, I know, the payoff will be worth every sacrifice.

# EPILOGUE

Coming clean has proven to be just as life changing as I had expected it would be. Since writing this book, I have lost my marriage. In the end, the real me just didn't mesh with him. We couldn't find a way to work through my deceit and all the confusion it caused. My ex-husband kept the house and most of the remaining material possessions we had accumulated, but I have my daughter, the dogs, and my new career. I couldn't be happier.

I no longer suffer from panic attacks, and I wake up each day able to look in the mirror and know who I am. I have good days and bad days, just like everyone else, but even my worst days are better than my best days back when I was a phony. I appreciate life, and I have found love.

Badger is back in my life—his marriage did not survive either. We don't stack up financially as we did before, but neither of us cares one bit. What I took away from my experience is that life morphs as time marches on, and things that are real have staying power.

My life is not what I expected it to be ten years ago. I am not a millionaire, I don't drive a sports car, and I am not a hotshot. But I am happy. I giggle now; I gush over things I love. I can lie on the beach and enjoy those moments. I can no longer afford the lavish vacations I could before, but I don't *need* them anymore.

My Happy Pie is finally balanced. My family gets what they need from me, and I get what I need from them. I know romantic love for the first time in my life. I enjoy my career and keep my schedule in check. My finances are status quo, and I am okay with that. I am ordinary, and I am okay with that too. I smile a lot.

My trip around this whirly-whirl is proving to be quite agreeable. I maintain my honesty about everything, even in situations where a white lie may serve the greater good. My honesty—my *integrity*—is not something I am willing to compromise ever again. And the people remaining in my life appreciate and understand that.